Sanjeev Kapoor's

NO-OIL
Vegetarian Cooking

In association with Alyona Kapoor

PopulaR prakashan

www.popularprakashan.com

Published by
POPULAR PRAKASHAN PVT. LTD.
301, Mahalaxmi Chambers
22, Bhulabhai Desai Road
Mumbai - 400026
for KHANA KHAZANA PUBLICATIONS PVT. LTD.

ISBN 978-81-7991-292-8
(4040)

Book Design   :   Creative Quotient (CQ-A Repro India
                        Limited Enterprise)
Photography   :   Mangesh Parab
Food Stylist   :   Harpal Singh Sokhi
Nutritionists   :   Prachi Hatwalne &
                        Kirti Masurkar

Printed in India
by Nutech Photolithographers
B-240, Okhla Industrial Area, Phase-I
New Delhi 110020

Author's Note

*L*ife is more fun and interesting if there is a challenge before you. This book was definitely interesting to write and of course challenging because my focus was totally on making oil-free food look great and taste good. And believe me, gone are the morose days when oil-free meant boiled steamed food with a dash of salt and pepper. It does not mean *khichdi* and *dahi* any more. Mealtimes are eminently more fulfilling if there is some access to recipes that you can enjoy along with the family given the fact that the food has to be oil-free.

A lot has been said and written about "low oil" or "no oil" diets, but how well the subject has been understood is the moot question. Modern life brings with it loads of stress, tension and related health problems. The progress in science has introduced various gadgets and means to relieve physical strain but then that very relief has given rise to ailments : though we have adjusted to the modern way of life we have not really been able to adjust our diet accordingly. The idea for this book took seed from here and you would be interested to know about the making of this book. I should say let us forget the journey but enjoy the final destination: in other words, my recipes are for everyday cooking. In this day and age when middle age diseases referred to so nonchalantly as 'lifestyle diseases' are on the rise, I am sure some of you would welcome this new addition to the kitchen. There are recipes for all courses in a meal, and each of them has been totally researched and perfected.

Oil has always been an important constituent of most cuisines around the world for it not only adds taste, but also imparts its own flavour. For example, coconut oil, olive oil, mustard oil etc. But along with the flavours comes the high fat content and the dense calories which are restricted for some of us for medical reasons. As you go along the book you will see that we have tried not to use any oil or ghee or cream or even certain ingredients with a high fat content. But at the same time, great care has been taken to ensure that the taste factor has not been much affected.

These recipes are meant not only for weight-watchers, they are for you and me who are health conscious, who want to look better, live better and longer! My mantra is to eat well but sensibly and follow a regular exercise regime. These recipes are suggestions to bring a change into the daily diet and by all means, use them whenever the need is to try out oil-free cooking.

Each active person is allowed 15 grams of visible fat a day. But the truth is that we end up having a lot more than the allowed quantity because most of us are unaware that all foods contain some percentage of fat. Be it wheat, pulses, vegetables, fruits, skimmed milk, cottage cheese, yogurt, cloves, cinnamon, sesame seeds and even the miniscule single mustard seed! So if we do eat a variety of foods each day, in a variety of menus, balancing the carbohydrate and protein intake, all invisible fat included in this way is just perfect for a healthy diet. My point here is that "no oil" does not mean that the food is totally free of lipid content.

It is important to keep the taste buds pampered because they rule the roost! The contents of this book do just that. All the recipes are written to provide for four portions. The portion size has been set keeping in mind that they form part of a menu which will have other complementary dishes and will be shared by a group of people.

So just tie up your aprons and armed with non-stick cookware try out this wonderful array of dishes that will not only help you live a healthy life but will also win hearts along the way.

Happy Cooking!

From Our Nutritionists' Desk

The purpose of giving you these oil free recipes is to bring some newness to your daily diet. We live in a world that is moving at breakneck speed. And in this stressed style of living, more and more people face the problem of raised cholesterol levels. And if this is not scary enough, we have life style diseases like obesity, diabetes and hypertension. Hence the pressing needs to decrease the intake of oil and fats.

The Need of the Hour

It would be perfectly correct to say that high cholesterol levels are also a result of a lack of exercise and regard for good health. Lack of time causes neglect of things that matter: like looking after one own's self, following a healthy eating pattern and also incorporating an exercise schedule into one's daily routine. Now is the time to tighten our belts simply because more and more young people seem to be suffering from all sorts of life style diseases that shorten life spans. This book presents a gentle guideline for eating low fat food, which is made without the addition of seed extracted oil.

Learn to Switch

Many people wonder about the pros and cons of an oil free diet. The important fact to remember is that we cannot do without oil. But we can certainly do with less oil in our food. And the sooner we adopt a fat free mode of cooking the better for our health in the long run. One weak moment of hunger that made you demolish a samosa adds a whopping 369 calories to your day's intake. Or have a small 105 grams pack of your favourite French fries, which will add 360 calories. Instead, two idlis will provide only 60 calories and be just as filling. Small things make a difference: switching over from buffalo's milk to cow's milk saves up to 50 calories and 2.4 grams of fat per 100 grams. The time has come to make your choices.

It is not really an Oil-Free World

You will realize while browsing through the book that we have not used any visible oil in the recipes. One can easily be led to think that an oil-free world exists. But it does not. The fact is, all foods contain some trace of oil fat like poppy seeds, coriander seeds, cumin seeds, cloves, peppercorns, sesame seeds and turmeric powder do have some fat content. These ingredients have been used in almost all the recipes ensuring that they are not misjudged as being 'fat free'. They are `low fat' and there are no great health hazards in having low fat foods. For those who are concerned it would be interesting to know that a hundred grams of poppy seeds contain 19.3 grams of fat. Similarly, cashew nuts, groundnuts, dried coconut, fresh coconut, almonds and walnuts also have considerable amounts of fat. Well, even arhar/toovar dal has a fat content - 100 grams has 1.5 grams of fat as compared to 3.7 in a moong dal preparation. Dals are not eaten raw and once they are cooked they do have additions of seeds and spices.

We Do Need Oil

Our bodily functions operate at the optimum when they are lubricated well and for all this all naturally present oils are good. We are all aware that oil adds taste and an appetizing appearance to anything you make. Yes, even some salads taste better with a dash of salad oil or olive oil. Oil is an integral part of most recipes because it removes the unpalatability of the dish and adds the needed softness, flavour and nutrients.

Some reasons why we need fat:

- Fat is a concentrated source of energy and is essential for the absorption of fat soluble vitamins.
- It is an important constituent of cells and helps in growth and development.
- Fat consists of Essential Fatty Acids (EFA). A no-fat diet deprives the body of these EFA and it could lead to growth retardation, skin lesions and liver degeneration. Dryness and scaliness of skin have also been observed.
- EFA are so named because they cannot be processed or manufactured by the body. They play an important role in growth, reproduction, skin and hair conditions and healing of wounds. They also play a structural role in cell membranes.

Weight loss and no-fat go together. But a long term no-fat diet is undesirable as it can lead to some serious problems like :

- Dry, itchy and scaling skin
- Dry, dull and and dandruff-ridden hair
- Poor healing of wounds
- Neurological disease
- Heart disease (arteriosclerosis)
- Skin diseases
- Degenerative conditions such as cataract, arthritis and cancer.

It is better to follow a diet that is low in fat but healthy in essential proteins, carbohydrates, vitamins and minerals. A good diet is primarily what we should be looking at. Hence this book of recipes that have been made without oil. If you have binged one day, the following day or two try making use of the recipes in this book.

And remember...
Eat sensibly, exercise and have a long and healthy life!

Contents

INGREDIENTS

2 teaspoons tea leaves

16 fresh mint leaves

4 lemons, cut into wedges

2 inches cinnamon

4 star anise (*chakri phool*)

16 teaspoons caster sugar

Mint Tea

1 Place tea leaves, mint leaves, lemon wedges, cinnamon, star anise and caster sugar in a teapot.

2 Pour boiling water, cover the teapot and allow to infuse for about three to four minutes. Stir well to dissolve the sugar. Pour into individual glasses and serve hot.

| Veg | Preparation 6 mins | Cooking 5 mins | Serves 4 people |

INGREDIENTS

4 kiwi fruit

¼ cup fresh mint leaves, chopped

¼ cup fresh coriander leaves, chopped

½ teaspoon cumin seeds, roasted

½ inch piece ginger, chopped

5-6 black peppercorns

3 tablespoons sugar

Salt to taste

1 teaspoon black salt

1 tablespoon lemon juice

Crushed ice, as required

Kiwi
ka Panna

1 Roast kiwi fruit in a tandoor or in an oven at 150⁰C/300⁰F/Gas Mark 2 for half an hour or till soft. Cool, peel and crush in a bowl with your fingers or with a wooden spoon, to a smooth pulp. Grind mint leaves, coriander leaves, cumin seeds, ginger and peppercorns to a smooth paste.

2 Blend kiwi pulp with sugar, salt, black salt and lemon juice. Add mint-coriander paste and mix well. Strain. Add four cups of water and stir well to mix. Put some ice cubes into individual glasses, pour the *panna* over and serve chilled.

| Veg | Preparation 30 mins | Cooking 10 mins | Serves 4 people |

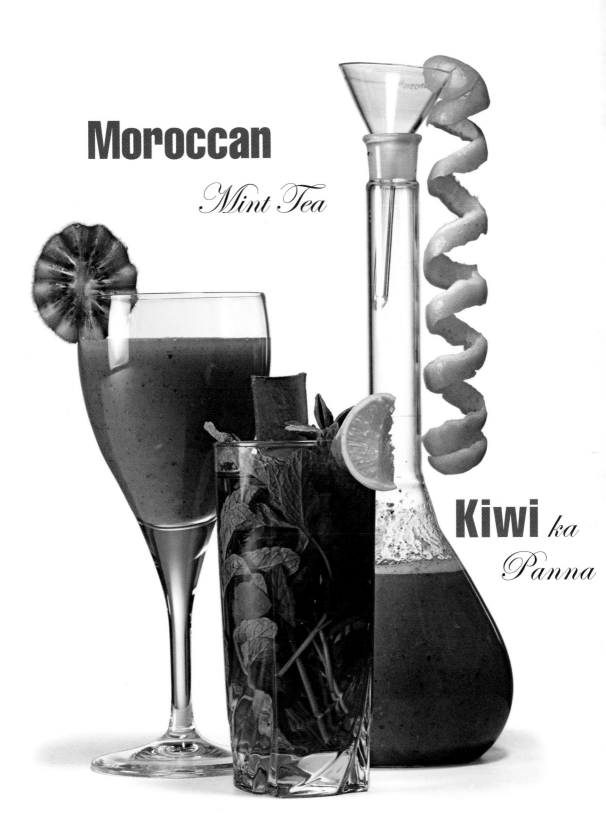

Moroccan *Mint Tea*

Kiwi *ka* *Panna*

INGREDIENTS

4 large black carrots (*kali gajar*)

4 tablespoons mustard seeds, coarsely powdered

3 tablespoons salt

1½ tablespoons coarse red chilli powder

Chef's Tip: If black carrots are not available, try the same kanji with red carrots. But try you must!

Kale Gajar
ki Kanji

1 Scrub carrots and wash under running water. Peel and cut carrots into batons. Take eighteen cups of water in a large jar or a clay pot (*matka*), which will be able to hold four litres of water. Add carrots, mustard powder, salt and red chilli powder and mix well.

2 Cover the pot with a piece of muslin and tie it around the rim. Let it stand in the sun for three to four days. Refrigerate when ready. Stir well before serving. Pour into tall glasses with pieces of carrot. Serve chilled.

Veg | Preparation 10 mins | Maturing 3-4 days | Serves 4 people

INGREDIENTS

2 medium cucumbers, peeled and roughly chopped

2 inch celery stalk, roughly chopped

2 tablespoons lemon juice

1 tablespoon sugar

Salt to taste

Ice cubes

FOR GARNISHING

A few sprigs of fresh mint leaves

4 three-inch long celery stalks

Tangy *Cucumber*
and Celery *Juice*

1 Put cucumber, celery, lemon juice, sugar and salt with four cups of water and ice cubes into a blender and process till well blended.

2 Pour the juice into glasses and serve immediately garnished with a sprig of mint and a celery stalk.

Veg | Preparation 10 mins | Making 5 mins | Serves 4 people

INGREDIENTS

½ cup split pigeon peas (*toovar/arhar dal*)

2 tablespoons split green gram with skin (*chilkewali moong dal*)

2 medium carrots

2-3 whole dried red chillies

6-8 black peppercorns

1 teaspoon cumin seeds

1 teaspoon coriander seeds

4-5 garlic cloves

2 green chillies, slit

Salt to taste

2 tablespoons fresh coriander leaves, chopped

Dal aur Gajar

Shorba

---

1 Soak *toovar dal* in two cups of water and *chilkewali moong dal* in half a cup of water, separately, for half an hour. Drain.

2 Cut one carrot roughly and grate the other coarsely. Dry roast whole red chillies, black peppercorns, cumin seeds and coriander seeds and grind together to a coarse powder.

3 Put the *dals* in a pressure cooker. Add the roughly cut carrot, garlic and three cups of water and cook till the *dals* are cooked completely.

4 Mash the *dals* with a hand blender till smooth. Add one cup of water and green chillies and bring to a boil. Add the ground spices and salt. Simmer for two minutes.

5 Serve garnished with coriander leaves and grated carrot.

Veg

Preparation 30 mins

Cooking 30 mins

Serves 4 people

11

INGREDIENTS

20-24 medium tomatoes, quartered

24 fresh basil leaves

2 bay leaves

20 black peppercorns

2 medium onions, sliced

8 garlic cloves, chopped

2 six-inch celery stalks, finely chopped

2 medium carrots, roughly chopped

Salt to taste

2 tablespoons gram flour (*besan*)

2 teaspoons sugar

Tomato
and Basil Soup

1 Heat a non-stick pan. Add bay leaves, half the peppercorns and onions and roast until the onions turn translucent.

2 Add garlic, celery and three tablespoons of water. Stir and add carrots and tomatoes.

3 Reserve six basil leaves for garnishing and add the rest to the tomatoes. Stir and add salt.

4 Cook on medium heat till the tomatoes soften. Add three cups of water and bring to a boil. Cover and cook for ten to fifteen minutes.

5 Pass mixture through a strainer and reserve the liquid. Remove peppercorns and bay leaves from the residue and allow it to cool. Process in a blender to get a smooth purée.

6 Roast gram flour in another pan till fragrant. Add the puréed tomatoes and mix. Add reserved liquid and adjust consistency.

7 Place the pan on heat. Add sugar, salt, remaining peppercorns, freshly crushed, and let the soup simmer for a couple of minutes. Strain and bring to a boil again.

8 Garnish with the reserved basil leaves and serve piping hot.

Veg

Preparation
15 mins

Cooking
25 mins

Serves
4 people

Tomato *and* Basil

Soup

INGREDIENTS

5 medium bananas, roughly chopped

5 tablespoons honey

2 tablespoons lemon juice

2 cups drained skimmed milk yogurt

10 ice cubes

10 fresh mint leaves, torn

Banana

and Honey Smoothie

1   Place roughly chopped bananas in a freezer for one hour. Place the frozen banana pieces, honey, lemon juice and yogurt in a blender and blend until smooth.

2   Add ice cubes and blend again. Pour into individual glasses and serve garnished with mint leaves.

| Veg | Preparation 1 hr | Making 5 mins | Serves 4 people |

INGREDIENTS

½ small musk melon, cut into ½ inch cubes

6 oranges

½ medium watermelon, seeded and roughly chopped

½ teaspoon *chaat masala*

Musk Melon

in Orange Juice

1   Squeeze out juice of oranges. Strain and set aside. Blend watermelon pieces in a blender till smooth. Strain.

2   Mix orange juice and watermelon juice. Add *chaat masala* and mix well. Chill.

3   To serve, put one-fourth of the musk melon cubes in each serving glass and pour the blended juice over.

4   Serve immediately.

| Veg | Preparation 10 mins | Making 10 mins | Serves 4 people |

INGREDIENTS

1 large apple, diced

½ medium fresh pineapple, diced

2 medium oranges, segmented

10 fresh mint leaves

FOR THE DRESSING

1 tablespoon lemon juice

1 teaspoon sugar

Salt to taste

½ teaspoon roasted cumin seeds, crushed

½ teaspoon red chilli flakes

5-6 black peppercorns, crushed

Apple, *Pineapple* and **Orange** *Salad*

1   Mix together all the ingredients for the dressing along with two tablespoons of water.

2   Mix together prepared apple, pineapple and orange. Add the dressing and toss well to mix.

3   Serve garnished with roughly torn mint leaves.

 Veg

 Preparation 10 mins

 Making 5 mins

 Serves 4 people

Red Capsicum

Soup with Lemon

Apple, Pineapple and Orange

Salad

INGREDIENTS

8 medium red capsicums

4 tablespoons lemon juice

2 medium onions, chopped

12 garlic cloves, chopped

1 tablespoon refined flour (*maida*)

5 cups Vegetable Stock (pg. 104)

4-5 fresh basil leaves

Salt to taste

1 teaspoon sugar

5-6 black peppercorns, crushed

Red Capsicum

Soup with Lemon

1   Prick red capsicums with a fork, and roast them directly on a low flame till lightly charred. Plunge into cold water, remove skin and chop roughly.

2   Put onions and garlic into a non-stick pan and roast on medium heat for a minute. Add refined flour and continue to roast for another minute till lightly browned or till it emits a pleasant aroma.

3   Add one cup of vegetable stock, the capsicums and a couple of fresh basil leaves. Stir and bring to a boil. Cover and simmer for three to four minutes. Cool and blend to a smooth purée.

4   Transfer into a thick-bottomed pan, add the remaining stock and bring to a boil.

5   Reduce heat, add salt, sugar and crushed peppercorns. Simmer for two to three minutes.

6   Add lemon juice, stir and pour into individual soup bowls. Serve hot, garnished with remaining fresh basil leaves.

 Veg

 Preparation 15 mins

 Cooking 20 mins

 Serves 4 people

INGREDIENTS

15-20 garlic cloves

2 tablespoons split pigeon peas (*toovar/arhar dal*), soaked

1 medium tomato, chopped

2 teaspoons tamarind pulp

Salt to taste

A pinch of asafoetida

¼ teaspoon turmeric powder

FOR THE RASAM POWDER

1 teaspoon cumin seeds

6-8 black peppercorns

4 whole red chillies

1 tablespoon coriander seeds

1 teaspoon split Bengal gram (*chana dal*)

FOR TEMPERING

½ teaspoon mustard seeds

2 whole red chillies

1 sprig curry leaves

Garlic-flavoured

Rasam

---

1   Heat a non-stick pan. Roast garlic cloves for a minute. Remove and set aside.

2   Boil three cups of water in a deep pan. Add *dal* and tomato and cook, covered, till soft. Mash and reserve along with the water.

3   Make the *rasam* powder : In a non-stick pan dry roast cumin seeds, peppercorns, whole red chillies, coriander seeds and split Bengal gram to a light brown colour. Cool and pound to a fine powder.

4   Add three more cups of water to the tamarind pulp and boil with salt, asafoetida, turmeric powder and the *rasam* powder for five minutes or till the raw smell of the tamarind disappears.

5   Add mashed *dal* to the *rasam* and bring to a boil. Reduce heat and simmer for five minutes. Strain and bring to a boil again.

6   For tempering, dry roast mustard seeds, red chillies and curry leaves in a non-stick pan and add to the strained *rasam*. Cover immediately to trap the flavours and serve piping hot, garnished with roasted garlic.

Chef's Tip: You can pound the garlic very lightly before adding to give a better and stronger flavour. Increase or decrease the garlic to suit your taste.

Veg

Preparation 10 mins

Cooking 30 mins

Serves 4 people

INGREDIENTS

6-8 fresh button mushrooms, sliced

½ medium carrot, thinly sliced

4-6 leaves Chinese cabbage,
 cut into 1 inch pieces

1 inch celery stalk, diagonally sliced

1 spring onion, sliced

1 medium red capsicum, seeded,
 cut into 1 inch pieces

8-10 snow peas, halved

12-16 spinach leaves, chopped

4-5 cups Vegetable Stock (pg. 104)

2-3 garlic cloves, crushed

¼ teaspoon MSG (optional)

3-4 black peppercorns, crushed

Salt to taste

½ cup bean sprouts

½ teaspoon lemon juice (optional)

Clear
Vegetable Soup

1 Heat vegetable stock in a wok or a pan, add crushed garlic and bring to a boil. Add mushrooms, carrot, Chinese cabbage, celery, spring onion, red capsicum, snow peas and spinach and cook for two to three minutes after it starts boiling again.

2 Add MSG, crushed peppercorns, salt and bean sprouts. Stir in lemon juice and serve piping hot.

Veg

Preparation
15 mins

Cooking
10 mins

Serves
4 people

Tropical Fruit

Salad

INGREDIENTS

2 medium oranges, separated
  into segments

2 medium sweet limes, separated
  into segments

1 medium apple, cut into
  ½ inch cubes

¼ small papaya, cut into
  ½ inch cubes

½ cup seedless grapes, (black
  and green)

1 medium guava, cut into
  ½ inch cubes

2 tablespoons lemon juice

2 tablespoons honey

1 teaspoon red chilli flakes

Black salt to taste

Tropical Fruit

Salad

1 Make a dressing with lemon juice, honey, red chilli
      flakes and black salt.

2 Mix the prepared fruit together in a big bowl, pour
      the dressing over and toss well to mix.

3 Serve chilled.

 Veg   Preparation
10 mins   Making
5 mins   Serves
4 people

INGREDIENTS

400 grams fresh button mushrooms, quartered

Salt to taste

2 teaspoons garlic paste

5-6 fresh basil leaves

5 tablespoons sugar

2 teaspoons balsamic vinegar

7-8 black peppercorns, crushed

Mushrooms

in Balsamic Vinegar

1 Marinate mushrooms in a mixture of salt, garlic paste and roughly torn basil leaves for two hours.

2 Heat sugar in a pan. Add one tablespoon of water, stir continuously till it caramelises to a light golden colour.

3 Add balsamic vinegar and crushed peppercorns and cook for three to four minutes.

4 Toss mushrooms in caramelised sugar mixture and refrigerate.

5 Serve chilled.

 Veg
 Preparation 2 hrs
 Cooking 10 mins
 Serves 4 people

INGREDIENTS

- 1 slice brown bread, toasted, cut into 1 inch pieces
- 2 medium onions
- 1 medium green capsicum, seeded, cut into 1 inch pieces
- 2 medium tomatoes, seeded, cut into 1 inch pieces
- 1 small head iceberg lettuce, torn into bite-size pieces
- 2 tablespoons brown breadcrumbs, toasted

FOR THE DRESSING

- 2 tablespoons vinegar
- Salt to taste
- 7-8 black peppercorns, crushed
- 6 small pickled gherkins, chopped
- 1 teaspoon dried rosemary
- ¼ teaspoon mixed herbs

Bread Salad

with Roasted Onions

1   Roast onions over an open flame. Cut into one inch square pieces.

2   For the dressing mix together vinegar, salt, crushed peppercorns, pickled gherkins, rosemary and mixed herbs.

3   Mix together bread cubes, onions, capsicum, tomato and iceberg lettuce in a bowl.

4   Just before serving, add the dressing and toss to mix. Garnish with toasted brown breadcrumbs and serve immediately.

 Veg
 Preparation 10 mins
 Cooking 5 mins
 Serves 4 people

INGREDIENTS

1 medium zucchini, peeled

2 medium carrots, peeled

2 medium cucumbers, peeled

Salt to taste

5 black olives, sliced

FOR THE DRESSING

2 tablespoons vinegar

1 tablespoon soy sauce

1 teaspoon brown sugar

¼ teaspoon red chilli flakes

3-4 fresh basil leaves

Vegetable

Ribbon Salad

1   Take a potato peeler or a manual slicer and slice zucchini, carrots and cucumbers lengthways into thin ribbons. Sprinkle a little salt and set aside for five minutes.

2   Blend vinegar, soy sauce, brown sugar, red chilli flakes, roughly torn basil leaves and salt to make a coarse paste. Transfer to a bowl.

3   Squeeze the cut vegetables to remove excess liquid.

4   Add vegetables to the dressing in the bowl and toss well.

5   Serve garnished with olive slices.

Veg	Preparation 10 mins	Making 5 mins	Serves 4 people

Vegetable

Ribbon Salad

Aloo Kachalu

Chaat

INGREDIENTS

2 large potatoes, boiled, peeled and cut into 1 inch cubes

1 large sweet potato, boiled, peeled and cut into 1 inch cubes

1½ tablespoons lemon juice

Salt to taste

1 inch ginger, cut into fine strips

1 large ripe banana

2 tablespoons tamarind pulp

2 green chillies, finely chopped

1 teaspoon *chaat masala*

2 tablespoons fresh coriander leaves, finely chopped

Aloo Kachalu

Chaat

1 Add half a teaspoon of lemon juice and a pinch of salt to ginger strips. Refrigerate.

2 Peel and cut banana into one inch pieces, mix with half a teaspoon of lemon juice and set aside.

3 Place potatoes, sweet potato and banana in a mixing bowl. Add remaining lemon juice, tamarind pulp, green chillies, *chaat masala*, salt to taste and coriander leaves; toss lightly.

4 Serve garnished with chilled pickled ginger strips.

Veg

Preparation 15 mins

Making 5 mins

Serves 4 people

INGREDIENTS

8-10 baby potatoes

10-12 French beans, cut into
1 inch pieces

½ teaspoon paprika or crushed
red chilli

FOR THE DRESSING

2 tablespoons *paneer* (made from
skimmed milk), crumbled

½ cup skimmed milk yogurt

1 teaspoon mustard paste

Salt to taste

7-8 black peppercorns, crushed

2 stalks spring onion greens,
chopped

Warm Potato Salad

with Green Beans

1 Boil potatoes in two cups of water, drain and set aside. Boil French beans in one cup of water, drain and refresh in cold water. Set aside.

2 Mix together baby potatoes leaving the skin on, and French beans and set aside.

3 For the dressing, mix *paneer*, yogurt, mustard paste, salt, crushed peppercorns and spring onion greens.

4 Fold the baby potatoes and French beans into the prepared dressing. Adjust seasoning.

5 Sprinkle paprika or crushed red chilli on top and serve.

 Veg Preparation 15 mins Cooking 10 mins Serves 4 people

INGREDIENTS

1 cup fresh corn kernels

1 large onion, finely chopped

1 large tomato, finely chopped

2 medium potatoes, boiled,
 cut into ½ inch cubes

2 teaspoons *chaat masala*

3-4 green chillies, finely chopped

2 tablespoons Green Coriander
 Chutney (see Note)

2 tablespoons Date and
 Tamarind Chutney (pg. 93)

4 tablespoons fresh coriander
 leaves, finely chopped

1½ teaspoons lemon juice

Salt to taste

1 cup cornflakes, crushed

Corn
Bhel

1 Bring three cups of water to a boil. Add the corn kernels and continue to boil for three to four minutes. Drain and remove excess water. This *bhel* can be made with hot or cold corn kernels.

2 Mix together the corn, onion, tomato, potatoes, *chaat masala*, green chillies, green coriender chutney, date and tamarind chutney and coriander leaves. Add lemon juice, salt and toss to mix.

3 Divide into individual servings, sprinkle cornflakes and serve immediately.

Note: Grind together 1 cup fresh coriander leaves, ½ cup fresh mint leaves, 2-3 green chillies, black salt to taste, ¼ teaspoon sugar and 1 tablespoon lemon juice to a smooth paste using a little water if required.

 Veg
 Preparation 10 mins
 Cooking 5 mins
 Serves 4 people

INGREDIENTS

FOR THE CHEELA

2 cups gram flour (*besan*)

¼ teaspoon soda bicarbonate

Salt to taste

1 teaspoon red chilli powder

1 teaspoon carom seeds (*ajwain*)

A pinch of asafoetida

2 tablespoons fresh coriander
leaves, chopped

FOR THE STUFFING

2 medium onions, chopped

1 cup fresh fenugreek leaves
(*methi*), chopped

8-10 fresh button mushrooms, sliced

2½ cups skimmed milk cottage
cheese (*paneer*), grated

Salt to taste

¼ teaspoon black pepper powder

Stuffed Methi
Cheela

1   For the stuffing heat a non-stick *kadai* and roast onions for two minutes. Add *methi* and cook for another minute. Add mushrooms, stir and cook till all the water dries up. Add cottage cheese, salt and pepper powder. Mix well and set aside to cool.

2   In a bowl, mix together gram flour, soda bicarbonate, salt, red chilli powder, carom seeds, asafoetida, coriander leaves and sufficient water to make a batter of pouring consistency. Whisk well to ensure there are no lumps.

3   Heat a non-stick pan, pour a ladleful of batter into the pan and spread it evenly. Cook the *cheela* on both sides.

4   Place a portion of the stuffing in the centre, fold the edges over and serve immediately.

Veg

Preparation
10 mins

Cooking
15 mins

Serves
4 people

Corn

Bhel

Stuffed Methi

Cheela

INGREDIENTS

FOR THE TACOS

¼ cup maize flour (*makai ka atta*)

4 teaspoons refined flour (*maida*)

A small pinch of turmeric powder

Salt to taste

FOR THE FILLING

2 medium potatoes, peeled and quartered

½ cup green peas, shelled

5-6 French beans, strings removed

1 medium carrot, cut into four pieces

¼ teaspoon turmeric powder

Salt to taste

1 large onion, finely chopped

3-4 garlic cloves, finely chopped

1 teaspoon red chilli paste

2 tablespoons tomato ketchup

½ cup bean sprouts

1 head of lettuce, shredded

Vegetable
Tacos

1   Mix all the ingredients for the tacos, add sufficient water and knead into a medium soft dough. Keep covered with a damp cloth for about fifteen minutes.

2   Divide into sixteen equal portions and roll into thin *puris*. Prick the *puris* with a fork.

3   Heat a non-stick tawa. Dry roast the *puris* on both sides. Fold over a rolling pin while still hot into a half-moon shape. Set aside to cool.

4   Boil potatoes, peas, French beans and carrot in sufficient water with turmeric powder and salt till done. When cooked, drain, mash and set aside to cool.

5   Heat a non-stick pan. Roast onion for two minutes. Add garlic and roast for another minute.

6   Add red chilli paste, salt and tomato ketchup. Cook for two minutes.

7   Add mashed vegetables and cook for another five to eight minutes. Take off the heat and cool.

8   To serve, stuff taco shells with the prepared filling. Top with bean sprouts and lettuce leaves. Serve immediately.

Veg

Preparation
15 mins

Cooking
30 mins

Serves
4 people

INGREDIENTS

½ cup rice flour, sifted

8 tablespoons skimmed milk yogurt, whisked

Salt to taste

1 teaspoon green chilli paste

½ teaspoon ginger paste

½ teaspoon soda bicarbonate

8 banana leaves, cut into 5 inch squares or circles

FOR THE STUFFING

½ cup sprouted green gram (*ankurit moong*)

Salt to taste

3-4 black peppercorns, crushed

¼ teaspoon red chilli flakes

Rice

Panki

1 Put the rice flour into a bowl. Add yogurt and salt and mix well. Add green chilli paste and ginger paste and mix again. Add enough water to make a batter of pouring consistency. Add soda bicarbonate and mix. Cover and set aside to ferment for about two hours.

2 Mix all the ingredients for the stuffing together.

3 Heat a non-stick *tawa*.

4 Pour rice batter on each banana leaf, place the stuffing in the centre and fold the leaf into half. Place it on the *tawa* and cook for two to three minutes. Turn and cook the other side as well.

5 Serve the *panki* in the banana leaf.

 Veg   Preparation 2 hrs   Cooking 15 mins   Serves 4 people

INGREDIENTS

300 grams skimmed milk cottage
cheese (*paneer*), cut into ½ inch cubes

1 cup wholewheat flour (*atta*)

Salt to taste

3 medium onions, chopped

3 medium tomatoes, chopped

1 tablespoon ginger paste

1 tablespoon garlic paste

1 teaspoon Kashmiri red chilli powder

½ teaspoon turmeric powder

2 teaspoons coriander powder
(optional)

2 tablespoons lemon juice

TO SERVE

8 teaspoons Green Coriander
Chutney (pg. 29)

2 medium onions, sliced

Paneer

---

1   Mix wholewheat flour and salt, add sufficient water and knead into a firm dough. Cover and rest the dough for about fifteen minutes.

2   Heat a non-stick pan, add onions, tomatoes, ginger paste, garlic paste, salt, Kashmiri red chilli powder, turmeric powder, coriander powder and stir well to mix. Cook till everything blends well and the excess moisture has dried up. Stir in the lemon juice, and take the pan off the heat.

3   Add *paneer* cubes and mix lightly. Divide the filling into eight equal portions and set aside.

4   Divide the dough into eight equal portions and roll into *rotis*.

5   Heat a *tawa* and cook each *roti* till both sides are evenly cooked.

6   Spread a teaspoonful of green coriander chutney over each *roti*. Place a portion of *paneer* mixture at one end. Sprinkle some sliced onions and roll up the *roti*.

7   Wrap in aluminium foil and serve immediately.

Veg | Preparation 15 mins | Cooking 15 mins | Serves 4 people

Paneer

Frankie

Vegetable Seekh

Kebabs

INGREDIENTS

1 medium potato, boiled and mashed

1 medium carrot, grated

½ cup green peas, crushed

5-6 French beans, finely chopped

1 teaspoon ginger paste

1 teaspoon dried mango powder (*amchur*)

2 teaspoons *chaat masala*

3-4 green chillies, chopped

1½ tablespoons *chhunda*

3 tablespoons roasted *chana* powder

150 grams skimmed milk cottage cheese (*paneer*), grated

Salt to taste

Vegetable
Seekh *Kebabs*

1 Heat a non-stick *kadai*. Add ginger paste and cook for half a minute. Add mashed potato, carrot, green peas and French beans and cook for a few minutes, stirring continuously.

2 Add *amchur*, *chaat masala*, green chillies, *chhunda*, and roasted *chana* powder and continue to cook for two to three minutes.

3 Add cottage cheese and mix well. Add salt and mix again.

4 Divide into eight equal portions. Take each portion and press around a skewer in a cylindrical shape.

5 Heat a non-stick *tawa* and place the skewers on it. Cook on moderate heat, rotating the skewers from time to time so that the kebabs cook evenly all round, to a golden brown.

6 Serve hot with chutney of your choice.

Chef's Tip: *Chhunda is a sweet-sour pickle made of grated unripe green mangoes. A popular Gujarati accompaniment.*

Veg

Preparation
10 mins

Cooking
20 mins

Serves
4 people

Dahi

Idli

INGREDIENTS

1 cup parboiled rice (*ukda chawal*)

½ cup split black gram
(*dhuli urad dal*)

Salt to taste

2 cups skimmed milk yogurt, whisked

6 tablespoons honey

2 tablespoons Green Coriander
Chutney (pg. 29)

2 tablespoons Date and
Tamarind Chutney (pg. 93)

¼ teaspoon red chilli powder

½ teaspoon cumin powder

2 tablespoons fresh coriander
leaves, chopped

1 Wash rice and soak in three cups of water for at least two to three hours.

2 Wash and soak *dal* in two cups of water for the same length of time.

3 Drain and grind the rice to a slightly coarse texture. Use water as required to make a batter of dropping consistency. Drain and grind the *dal*, sprinkling water as required, to make a smooth and spongy batter.

4 Mix both the batters. Sprinkle salt and whip the mixture thoroughly with your fingers. Pour batter into a large vessel, close tightly with a lid and rest in a warm place overnight to ferment.

5 Heat sufficient water in a steamer.

6 Line the hollows of an *idli* stand with pieces of muslin. Pour a spoonful of the fermented batter into each hollow. Place the *idli* stand in the steamer. Steam for eight to ten minutes or till *idlis* are done.

7 Meanwhile, mix yogurt and honey thoroughly.

8 Place *idlis* in a serving bowl; drizzle sweetened yogurt, green coriander chutney and date and tamarind chutney over the *idlis*. Sprinkle red chilli powder and cumin powder.

9 Garnish with coriander leaves and serve.

 Veg Preparation 12 hrs Cooking 15 mins Serves 4 people

INGREDIENTS

6 medium potatoes

1 medium onion, finely chopped

Salt to taste

7-8 black peppercorns, ground coarsely

A pinch of nutmeg powder

2 tablespoons fresh parsley, chopped

Hash Brown
Potatoes

1   Boil potatoes in sufficient water till nearly done. They should be slightly undercooked. Peel and grate potatoes. Heat a non-stick pan. Add onion and roast till translucent. Remove from heat. Preheat oven to 200°C/400°F/Gas Mark 6. Mix grated potatoes and roasted onion along with salt, half the ground peppercorns and nutmeg powder.

2   Mix well and put in a baking tray and spread evenly with your fingers. Sprinkle the remaining ground peppercorns over the potatoes. Bake in the preheated oven for ten to fifteen minutes or till the potatoes turn light brown. Cut into wedges, garnish with parsley and serve hot.

INGREDIENTS

1 cup fine semolina (*rawa/suji*)

1 cup yogurt

Salt to taste

¼ teaspoon soda bicarbonate

1 medium onion, chopped

1 medium green capsicum, seeded and chopped

Red chilli powder, to taste

Crushed roasted cumin seeds, to taste

Instant
Uttappam

1   Put semolina in a bowl with yogurt and salt. Mix well and set aside for fifteen minutes. Add half a cup of water and soda bicarbonate and mix again.

2   Heat a non-stick *tawa* and pour a ladleful of batter in the centre. Do not spread the batter. Sprinkle onion, capsicum, red chilli powder and cumin seeds over the *uttappam* and allow to cook on moderate heat.

3   When the underside has cooked, flip over and cook the other side till set. Serve hot.

Veg

Preparation
10 mins

Cooking
20 mins

Serves
4 people

INGREDIENTS

200 grams yam (*suran*), cut into
1 inch pieces

2 medium potatoes, cut into
1 inch pieces

4 tablespoons split Bengal gram
(*chana dal*), soaked

1 large carrot, grated

10-12 French beans, finely chopped

¼ cup green peas, coarsely ground

1 teaspoon cumin seeds

1 inch ginger, finely chopped

2-3 green chillies, finely chopped

Salt to taste

2 tablespoons fresh coriander
leaves, chopped

¼ teaspoon turmeric powder

½ teaspoon *Garam Masala*
Powder (pg. 104)

½ teaspoon red chilli powder

5 teaspoons lemon juice

Vegetable
Shammi *Kebabs*

1   Drain *chana dal* and transfer to a pan. Add yam and potatoes and one and a half cups of water. Cover and cook till completely dry.

2   Heat a non-stick pan. Add cumin seeds and roast lightly. Add carrot, French beans, green peas, ginger, green chillies and salt and sauté on medium heat for two minutes. Transfer to a plate and cool.

3   Grind the *chana dal* mixture along with the sautéed vegetables to a smooth mixture.

4   Add coriander leaves, turmeric powder, *garam masala* powder, red chilli powder, and lemon juice and mix well. Adjust seasoning.

5   Divide this mixture into sixteen equal portions and shape into balls. Flatten lightly in the palm of your hand to form *kebabs*. Refrigerate for an hour.

6   Heat a non-stick pan and cook the *kebabs* till golden brown on both sides. Serve hot with Green Coriander Chutney (pg. 29).

Veg

Preparation
90 mins

Cooking
15 mins

Serves
4 people

Soya

Burger

INGREDIENTS

1 cup soya granules

2½ cups skimmed milk

4-5 medium potatoes, boiled
and mashed

1 medium onion, finely chopped

2 green chillies, finely chopped

2 tablespoons fresh coriander leaves,
finely chopped

¼ teaspoon cumin powder

1 teaspoon red chilli powder

¼ teaspoon clove powder

¼ teaspoon cinnamon powder

1½ teaspoons lemon juice

Salt to taste

¾ cup brown breadcrumbs

TO SERVE

4 burger buns

4 tablespoons mustard paste

4 tablespoons tomato ketchup

10-12 lettuce leaves

1 medium onion, sliced into rings

Soya
Burger

1   Soak soya granules in two cups of milk for fifteen
    minutes. Drain and squeeze out excess milk. Grind
    to mince the granules further.

2   In a large mixing bowl, mix together soya granules,
    mashed potatoes, onion, green chillies, coriander
    leaves, cumin powder, red chilli powder, clove
    powder, cinnamon powder, lemon juice and salt.

3   Divide the mixture into four equal portions. Shape
    each portion into a patty of three inches diameter
    and about half an inch thick.

4   Coat each patty evenly with breadcrumbs.

5   Heat a non-stick pan and cook the patties on both
    sides till crisp.

6   Halve a burger bun horizontally. Apply mustard paste
    on the lower half and tomato ketchup on the top half.
    Place two or three lettuce leaves on the lower half.
    Place the patty on it, top with onion rings, cover with
    the top half of the bun and serve immediately.

Veg   Preparation   Cooking   Serves
         20 mins   15 mins   4 people

INGREDIENTS

500 grams skimmed milk cottage
cheese (*paneer*)

2 tablespoons gram flour (*besan*)

¼ teaspoon turmeric powder

½ tablespoon ginger paste

½ tablespoon garlic paste

½ teaspoon white pepper powder

Salt to taste

2 tablespoons lemon juice

½ teaspoon green cardamom
powder

½ teaspoon Lucknowi fennel
(*saunf*) powder

A few strands of saffron (*kesar*)

1 cup thick skimmed milk
yogurt, drained

2 medium green capsicums,
seeded and cut into
1½ inch squares

1½ teaspoons *chaat masala*

Saunfia
Paneer Tikka

1 Wash and cut *paneer* into one and a half inch squares of half-inch thickness.

2 Heat a non-stick pan. Add gram flour and roast on moderate heat until it emits a pleasant aroma. Remove from heat and add turmeric powder. Cool and transfer to a bowl.

3 Add ginger paste, garlic paste, white pepper powder, salt, one tablespoon of lemon juice, green cardamom powder, fennel powder, saffron and yogurt. Whisk well to make a smooth batter.

4 Add *paneer* cubes to the batter and marinate for at least an hour.

5 Thread *paneer* cubes and capsicum squares alternately onto skewers.

6 Roast in a *tandoor*/charcoal grill for five minutes till the *tikkas* are golden in colour.

7 Alternatively, you can cook the *tikkas* in a convection oven or on a grill. Preheat the oven to 220⁰C/425⁰F/ Gas Mark 7 and cook the *tikkas* for three minutes on each side.

8 Remove and sprinkle with *chaat masala* powder and the remaining lemon juice. Serve with a chutney of your choice.

 Veg

 Preparation 20 mins

 Cooking 20 mins

 Serves 4 people

INGREDIENTS

8 colocasia leaves (*arbi patta*)

1½ cups gram flour (*besan*)

A pinch of asafoetida

2 teaspoons coriander powder

2 teaspoons cumin powder

1 teaspoon red chilli powder

1 teaspoon turmeric powder

2 teaspoons sesame seeds (*til*)

½ teaspoon soda bicarbonate

Salt to taste

2 teaspoons green chilli paste

2 teaspoons ginger paste

¼ teaspoon *Garam Masala* Powder (pg. 104)

4 tablespoons grated jaggery

2 tablespoons tamarind pulp

¼ cup scraped coconut

2 tablespoons fresh coriander leaves, chopped

Patra

1   Remove the thick stems of the leaves; wash, wipe dry and set aside.

2   In a large bowl mix together gram flour, asafoetida, coriander powder, cumin powder, red chilli powder and turmeric powder. Add sesame seeds, soda bicarbonate, salt, green chilli paste, ginger paste, *garam masala* powder, jaggery and tamarind pulp. Add three tablespoons of water and mix well.

3   Spread the paste evenly on the back of one leaf. Place another leaf over it and spread the paste evenly. Fold the two sides in and roll into six-inch rolls making sure that the paste does not ooze out.

4   Make similar rolls with the remaining colocasia leaves and gram flour paste.

5   Heat sufficient water in a steamer. Place the rolls on a perforated plate and steam for about thirty to forty minutes or till cooked. Insert a knife to check if done. (If the knife comes out clean, the *patra* is cooked). Remove and set aside to cool.

6   When cool, cut into half-inch thick round slices.

7   Serve hot, garnished with scraped coconut and coriander leaves.

Note: *You do not grate fresh coconut, you scrape it. You grate dried coconut (khopra).*

Chef's Tip: *When buying colocasia leaves choose ones which have dark, almost black stems. The ones with light stems may cause itching of the skin.*

| Veg | Preparation 20 mins | Cooking 40 mins | Serves 4 people |

INGREDIENTS

FOR THE COVERING

1 cup wholewheat flour (*atta*)

½ teaspoon carom seeds (*ajwain*)

Salt to taste

FOR THE STUFFING

½ cup shelled green peas

2 medium potatoes, cut into
½ inch cubes

1 teaspoon cumin seeds

1 inch ginger, finely chopped

3-4 green chillies, finely chopped

1 teaspoon red chilli powder

1 teaspoon dried mango powder
(*amchur*)

1 teaspoon *Garam Masala*
Powder (pg. 104)

Salt to taste

2 tablespoons fresh coriander
leaves, finely chopped

Baked

Samosas

1   Mix the ingredients for the covering; add one-third cup of water and knead into a stiff dough. Rest the dough covered with a damp cloth, for ten to fifteen minutes.

2   Cook green peas in one cup of boiling salted water till soft. Refresh in cold water and drain.

3   Heat a non-stick pan and lightly roast cumin seeds. Add ginger, green chillies, potatoes, red chilli powder, dried mango powder, *garam masala* powder and salt to taste; stir well to mix.

4   Sprinkle a little water over the mixture and cook, covered, till potatoes are done.

5   Add cooked green peas and cook for five minutes on low heat. Add coriander leaves and mix.

6   Let the mixture cool and divide into eight equal portions. Preheat the oven to 180°C/350°F/Gas Mark 4.

7   Divide the dough into four equal portions and roll into balls. Roll each ball into an elongated oval sheet.

8   Cut each sheet into half. Dampen the edges with water. Shape each half into a cone and stuff with a portion of the potato and pea filling. Seal the dampened edges well.

9   Arrange the *samosas* on a baking tray and bake for twenty to twenty-five minutes turning the *samosas* every five minutes.

10   Serve hot with Date and Tamarind Chutney (pg. 93).

| Veg | Preparation 15 mins | Cooking 40 mins | Serves 4 people |

Grilled Salt and Pepper Tofu
and Baked Samosas

INGREDIENTS

200 grams tofu, cut into ½ inch cubes

Sea salt to taste

2 spring onions, chopped

1 inch ginger, chopped

2 inch celery stalk, chopped

2 green chillies, chopped

3-4 garlic cloves, chopped

½ teaspoon black pepper powder

2 spring onion greens, chopped

Grilled Salt and Pepper Tofu

1 Sprinkle salt over tofu and mix lightly. Heat a non-stick frying pan till very hot. Add the tofu, it will brown instantly. Turn and cook the other side as well.

2 Remove the tofu and add spring onions, ginger, celery, green chillies and garlic to the same pan and stir-fry on high heat.

3 Add the browned tofu along with a little salt and black pepper powder and toss again to mix. Remove the pan from the heat. Sprinkle chopped spring onion greens, mix and serve immediately.

Veg | Preparation 10 mins | Cooking 5 mins | Serves 4 people

INGREDIENTS

2 cups fresh corn kernels, boiled

1 teaspoon red chilli flakes

1 green chilli, chopped

1 tablespoon lemon juice

1 small green capsicum, seeded and chopped

1 small red capsicum, seeded and chopped

Salt to taste

3-4 black peppercorns, crushed

2 tablespoons fresh coriander leaves, chopped

Hot Chilli Corn

1 Heat a non-stick pan. Add boiled corn kernels, red chilli flakes and green chilli and cook for a minute.

2 Add lemon juice, green capsicum, red capsicum and salt. Cover the pan and allow the vegetables to soften for about two minutes.

3 Mix well. Add crushed peppercorns and serve garnished with coriander leaves.

Veg | Preparation 10 mins | Cooking 5 mins | Serves 4 people

INGREDIENTS

40 baby potatoes

½ teaspoon turmeric powder

Salt to taste

1 cup fresh coriander leaves, roughly chopped

¼ cup fresh mint leaves, coarsely shredded

10-12 green chillies, coarsely chopped

4-6 garlic cloves, coarsely chopped

2 inches ginger, coarsely chopped

4 teaspoons lemon juice

2 teaspoons cumin seeds

2 teaspoons coriander powder

1 teaspoon cumin powder

½ cup skimmed milk yogurt

1 teaspoon sesame seeds (*til*), toasted

Chutneywale

Aloo

1 Parboil potatoes with salt and one-fourth teaspoon of turmeric powder. Drain, cool and halve without peeling.

2 For the chutney, grind coriander leaves, mint leaves, green chillies, garlic and ginger along with salt and lemon juice to a fine paste.

3 Heat a non-stick pan and dry roast cumin seeds till they emit a pleasant aroma. Add halved potatoes, coriander powder, cumin powder, remaining turmeric powder and mix well. Add half a cup of water, cover and cook on low heat till the potatoes are done.

4 Add the chutney, half a cup of water and stir to mix. Adjust salt and simmer for three to four minutes or till the gravy has thickened. Add yogurt and stir. Cook till the gravy comes to a boil and take off the heat.

5 Sprinkle toasted sesame seeds and serve hot.

Veg | Preparation 15 mins | Cooking 15 mins | Serves 4 people

Chutneywale

Aloo

Vegetable Stew *with*

Garlic Bread

INGREDIENTS

2 medium carrots, cut into
 1 inch pieces

¼ small cauliflower, separated
 into florets

¼ cup green peas, shelled

2 medium potatoes, cut into
 1 inch pieces

1 medium zucchini, cut into
 1 inch pieces

1 inch fresh ginger, sliced

3-4 cloves

8-10 black peppercorns

1 teaspoon cumin seeds

1 medium onion, sliced

4$\frac{1}{3}$ cups Vegetable Stock (pg. 104)

Salt to taste

1 stalk celery, cut into 1 inch pieces

3-4 black peppercorns, crushed

5 spinach leaves, shredded

1 loaf garlic bread, sliced

Vegetable *Stew*

with Garlic Bread

1   Blanch carrots, cauliflower and green peas
     individually in boiling water. Refresh in cold water
     and set aside.

2   Tie ginger, cloves, peppercorns and cumin seeds in
     a muslin cloth to make a *bouquet garni.*

3   Heat a non-stick pan. Add onion and roast lightly.
     Add vegetable stock and bring to a boil.

4   Put the *bouquet garni* into the boiling stock. Season
     with salt.

5   Add potatoes. Cover and cook over medium heat.
     Once the potatoes are cooked, remove the *bouquet
     garni* and mash the potatoes to thicken the stock.

6   Add celery, zucchini, carrots, cauliflower and green
     peas and cook on low heat for two minutes. Adjust
     salt and add crushed peppercorns.

7   Add spinach and mix well.

8   Lightly toast slices of garlic bread and serve with
     hot stew.

Veg   Preparation   Cooking   Serves
       20 mins   20 mins   4 people

INGREDIENTS

1 cup green peas, shelled

200 grams skimmed milk cottage
cheese (*paneer*), cut into
½ inch cubes

¾ teaspoon cumin seeds

2 large onions, finely chopped

1 tablespoon ginger-garlic paste

2 green chillies, chopped

¼ teaspoon turmeric powder

1 teaspoon red chilli powder

1 teaspoon coriander powder

2 large tomatoes, puréed

Salt to taste

¼ teaspoon *Garam Masala* Powder
(pg. 104)

1 tablespoon fresh coriander
leaves, chopped

Matar
Paneer

1 Heat a non-stick pan and add cumin seeds. When
they begin to change colour, add onions and ginger-
garlic paste. Cook till lightly browned. Add green
chillies, turmeric powder, red chilli powder and
coriander powder and one-third cup of water and
mix well.

2 Add tomato purée, salt and one cup of water. Cook
for two minutes. Add green peas and mix well. Cook
for five minutes or till peas are done.

3 Add *paneer* cubes and *garam masala* powder and
stir gently.

4 Serve hot garnished with coriander leaves.

Veg

Preparation
10 mins

Cooking
10 mins

Serves
4 people

INGREDIENTS

½ cup corn kernels, boiled

2 large bunches (600 grams each) spinach

2 medium onions, chopped

1 inch fresh ginger, grated

2 green chillies, chopped

A pinch of turmeric powder

1 teaspoon red chilli powder

1 teaspoon dried mango powder (*amchur*)

Salt to taste

¼ cup skimmed milk yogurt

1 teaspoon *Garam Masala* Powder (pg. 104)

1 teaspoon dried fenugreek leaves (*kasoori methi*), crushed

1 inch fresh ginger, cut into thin strips

Makai
Palak

1 Blanch spinach in sufficient boiling water for one minute. Drain and purée in a blender.

2 Heat a non-stick pan and roast onions, ginger and green chillies for two to three minutes.

3 Add turmeric powder, red chilli powder, dried mango powder and salt. Add one-fourth cup of water. Mix well and simmer for one or two minutes.

4 Add yogurt and mix well. Add spinach purée, corn kernels and salt and cook for two minutes.

5 Add *garam masala* powder and *kasoori methi*, stir and remove from heat.

6 Garnish with ginger strips and serve hot with *rotis*.

 Veg
 Preparation 15 mins
 Cooking 10 mins
 Serves 4 people

Thai Green Curry with
Vegetables

INGREDIENTS

1 medium carrot, cut into diamonds

½ small cauliflower, separated into small florets

2-3 baby brinjals

1 medium potato, cut into ½ inch cubes

5 stalks lemon grass

1 teaspoon lemon juice

Salt to taste

¾ cup fresh coconut milk

2-3 fresh basil leaves

GREEN CURRY PASTE

10 green chillies

3 shallots/*sambhar* onions

9 garlic cloves

1 inch galangal

3 inch stalk lemon grass

¼ teaspoon lemon rind, grated

A small bunch of coriander roots

2 teaspoons coriander seeds

2 teaspoons cumin seeds

Salt to taste

Thai Green

Curry with Vegetables

1 To make green curry paste, grind green chillies, shallots, garlic, galangal, lemon grass, lemon rind, coriander roots, coriander seeds, cumin seeds and salt to a fine paste.

2 Blanch all the vegetables individually in boiling water and refresh in cold water. Tie lemon grass in a piece of muslin to make a bundle. Crush it slightly.

3 Heat a non-stick pan, add green curry paste and roast for one minute. Add the blanched vegetables and lemon juice and cook for three to four minutes, stirring continuously.

4 Add three cups of water and continue to cook. Add lemon grass bundle and cook for three to four minutes till the curry absorbs its flavour.

5 Remove the lemon grass and add salt and coconut milk. Simmer for one minute.

6 Add basil leaves and take off the heat. Serve hot.

Chef's Tip: Galangal is a type of ginger used in Thai cooking. If not available use ginger.

Veg   Preparation 20 mins   Cooking 15 mins   Serves 4 people   53

INGREDIENTS

20 unpeeled baby potatoes

½ cup skimmed milk yogurt

A pinch of asafoetida

2 teaspoons garlic paste

2 teaspoons ginger paste

2 teaspoons red chilli powder

½ teaspoon turmeric powder

2 teaspoons coriander powder

1 teaspoon cumin powder

½ teaspoon *Garam Masala* Powder (pg. 104)

Salt to taste

2 large onions, chopped

2 tablespoons fresh coriander leaves, chopped

Baby Potatoes
in Spicy Yogurt Gravy

1 Parboil potatoes in sufficient water. Drain and set aside.

2 Mix together yogurt, asafoetida, garlic paste, ginger paste, red chilli powder, turmeric powder, coriander powder, cumin powder, *garam masala* powder and salt. Pierce unpeeled baby potatoes with a fork, add to the marinade and marinate for about half an hour.

3 Heat a non-stick pan and roast onions till lightly browned. Add baby potatoes along with the marinade and mix. Once the mixture comes to a boil, lower the heat and cook till the gravy thickens and coats the potatoes.

4 Garnish with coriander leaves and serve hot with *rotis*.

Veg | Preparation 30 mins | Cooking 10 mins | Serves 4 people

Main Course

INGREDIENTS

1 cup mixed sprouts
 (such as *moong, matki, chana*)

½ teaspoon mustard seeds

6-8 curry leaves

2 medium onions, finely chopped

½ teaspoon turmeric powder

½ teaspoon red chilli powder

1 teaspoon *Goda Masala* (pg. 104)

1 teaspoon jaggery, grated

Salt to taste

2 tablespoons fresh coriander
 leaves, finely chopped

2 tablespoons scraped coconut

FOR THE SPICE PASTE

6-7 garlic cloves

3-4 green chillies, roughly chopped

1 teaspoon cumin seeds, roasted

¼ cup scraped coconut

Mixed
Sprouts
Ussal

1 For the spice paste, grind garlic, green chillies, cumin seeds and scraped coconut to a smooth paste using little water if required.

2 Heat a non-stick pan, add mustard seeds and when they crackle add curry leaves and onions. Cook, stirring continuously till onions turn light golden.

3 Add ground paste and cook on moderate heat for three to four minutes.

4 Add turmeric powder, red chilli powder, *goda masala*, jaggery and salt. Stir well.

5 Add mixed sprouts, stir and add enough water to just cover the sprouts.

6 Bring to a boil and continue cooking on moderate heat, stirring occasionally, till the sprouts are cooked.

7 Serve hot garnished with coriander leaves and coconut.

 Veg Preparation 10 mins Cooking 15 mins Serves 4 people

INGREDIENTS

200 grams skimmed milk cottage
   cheese (*paneer*)

8-10 black peppercorns

2 inches cinnamon

5 green cardamoms

10 cloves

1 tablespoon ginger paste

1 tablespoon garlic paste

4-6 green chillies, chopped

2 cups tomato purée

1 teaspoon Kashmiri red chilli powder

1 teaspoon *Garam Masala*
   Powder (pg. 104)

Salt to taste

2 tablespoons honey

1 teaspoon dried fenugreek
   leaves (*kasoori methi*)

Paneer

---

1   Cut the *paneer* into one inch cubes or triangles.

2   Heat a non-stick pan. Add peppercorns, cinnamon, green cardamoms and cloves. Roast till they emit a pleasant aroma. Add ginger paste, garlic paste, green chillies and three tablespoons of water. Stir well and cook for two minutes.

3   Add tomato purée, red chilli powder, *garam masala* powder, salt and three cups of water. Bring to a boil, reduce heat and simmer for ten minutes.

4   Add honey and mix well. Strain the gravy and heat again. Stir in the crushed *kasoori methi*. Adjust salt and mix well.

5   Add the *paneer* and simmer for three to four minutes.

6   Serve hot.

 Veg   Preparation 20 mins   Cooking 20 mins   Serves 4 people

INGREDIENTS

1 cup soya granules

1 cup shelled green peas

1½ cups skimmed milk

2 medium onions, finely chopped

8 garlic cloves, finely chopped

1 inch ginger, grated

2 green chillies, chopped

1 teaspoon coriander powder

1 teaspoon cumin powder

¾ teaspoon red chilli powder

4 tablespoons fresh coriander
 leaves, chopped

Salt to taste

1 teaspoon *Garam Masala*
 Powder (pg. 104)

1 tablespoon lemon juice

Soya Keema

Matar

1 Soak soya granules in milk for an hour.

2 Heat a non-stick pan and add onions. Roast till lightly browned. Add garlic and roast for a minute.

3 Add ginger, green chillies, coriander powder, cumin powder, red chilli powder and two tablespoons of water. Stir and cook for two minutes.

4 Add green peas and one-fourth cup of water and mix well. Cover and cook till peas are nearly done.

5 Add soya granules along with the milk and cook till almost dry.

6 Add coriander leaves, salt, *garam masala* powder and lemon juice and mix well.

7 Serve hot.

 Veg Preparation 60 mins Cooking 20 mins Serves 4 people

Soya Keema

Matar

Gatta

Curry

INGREDIENTS

FOR THE GATTA

2½ cups gram flour (*besan*), sifted

3 tablespoons skimmed milk yogurt

½ teaspoon cumin seeds

½ teaspoon red chilli powder

½ teaspoon turmeric powder

Salt to taste

A pinch of soda bi-carbonate

FOR THE GRAVY

2 medium onions

½ inch ginger

1½ cups skimmed milk yogurt

1 teaspoon red chilli powder

2 teaspoons coriander powder

½ teaspoon turmeric powder

1 teaspoon cumin seeds

A pinch of asafoetida

Salt to taste

½ teaspoon *Garam Masala* Powder (pg. 104)

2 tablespoons fresh coriander leaves, chopped

Gatta

Curry

1   Mix all the ingredients for the *gatta*. Add sufficient water to make a stiff dough. Divide into six equal portions and roll into cylindrical shapes.

2   Cook the *gatta* in five cups of boiling hot water for ten to fifteen minutes. Drain and reserve the water for the gravy. Cut *gatta* diagonally into one inch pieces.

3   Roughly cut onions and boil in half a cup of water. Cool and grind with ginger to a fine paste.

4   Whisk yogurt with red chilli powder, coriander powder and turmeric powder.

5   Heat a non-stick pan. Add cumin seeds and asafoetida. Roast until cumin seeds start to change colour.

6   Add onion paste and cook on low heat till it turns light pink.

7   Add yogurt mixture and simmer for five minutes.

8   Add *gatta*, salt and one cup of the reserved water in which *gatta* were boiled. Simmer till gravy thickens. Add *garam masala* powder and adjust seasoning.

9   Garnish with coriander leaves and serve hot.

 Veg   Preparation 15 mins   Cooking 30 mins   Serves 4 people

INGREDIENTS

2 large bunches (600 grams each) spinach

4 medium potatoes

4 medium onions

8-10 garlic cloves, chopped

Salt to taste

7-8 black peppercorns, crushed

½ teaspoon Tabasco sauce

¾ cup skimmed milk

A pinch of nutmeg powder

½ cup brown breadcrumbs

Spinach
and Potato Bake

1   Blanch spinach in sufficient boiling water for one minute. Drain, refresh in cold water and chop.

2   Boil two potatoes, peel and mash till smooth. Peel and slice the remaining two potatoes into thin slices. Blanch in hot water for two to three minutes, drain and set aside. Chop two onions and slice the remaining two into rings.

3   Preheat the oven to 180°C/350°F/Gas Mark 4.

4   Heat a non-stick pan and roast chopped onions and garlic till light brown. Add spinach (first press it with your hands to remove excess water). Cook for a few minutes till all the water is absorbed. Add salt, half the crushed peppercorns and Tabasco sauce. Set aside.

5   Heat another non-stick pan. Toss the potato slices and onion rings together. Add salt and remaining crushed peppercorns and toss again.

6   Mix the mashed potatoes, milk and nutmeg powder together to a smooth mixture. Transfer into a piping bag with a star nozzle.

7   Take an ovenproof dish and layer the spinach mixture and potato and onion mixture in alternate layers. Sprinkle the breadcrumbs over the last layer. Pipe mashed potato rosettes on top and bake for thirty minutes. Serve hot.

| Veg | Preparation 20 mins | Cooking 40 mins | Serves 4 people |

INGREDIENTS

FOR THE *KOFTA*

1 small (250 grams) bottle gourd (*lauki*), peeled and grated

2 medium bunches (350 grams each) spinach

Salt to taste

3 medium potatoes, boiled and mashed

2-3 green chillies, finely chopped

1 tablespoon raisins (*kishmish*)

3 tablespoons coarse rice powder

½ teaspoon *chaat masala*

1 teaspoon ginger paste

1 teaspoon garlic paste

1 large onion, finely chopped

FOR THE CURRY

1 teaspoon ginger paste

1 teaspoon garlic paste

1 large onion, chopped

1 teaspoon red chilli powder

¼ teaspoon turmeric powder

½ teaspoon *Garam Masala* Powder (pg. 104)

1 teaspoon dried fenugreek leaves (*kasoori methi*), roasted and crushed

5-6 medium tomatoes, puréed

1½ tablespoons honey

2 tablespoons fresh coriander leaves, chopped

Steamed *Lauki* and *Palak Koftas*

1   Add salt to the grated bottle gourd and leave for five minutes. Squeeze bottle gourd to completely remove excess water. Blanch spinach in sufficient boiling water for one minute. Drain, refresh in cold water, squeeze out excess water and chop.

2   Combine the bottle gourd and spinach with potatoes, green chillies, raisins, rice powder, *chaat masala*, ginger paste, garlic paste, onion and salt in a large bowl. Divide into twenty equal portions and shape into oval *koftas*. Steam the *koftas* in a steamer for fifteen-twenty minutes. Set aside.

3   Heat a non-stick pan. Roast ginger paste, garlic paste and onion on medium heat for five to six minutes. Add red chilli powder, turmeric powder, *garam masala* powder, *kasoori methi* and two tablespoons of water and cook for a minute.

4   Add tomato purée, honey and salt. Add one cup of water and simmer for ten minutes. Arrange the steamed *koftas* on a serving plate, pour the gravy over and serve immediately garnished with coriander leaves.

 Veg
 Preparation 15 mins
 Cooking 30 mins
 Serves 4 people

Khumb
Hara Pyaaz

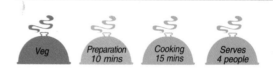

INGREDIENTS

40 fresh button mushrooms, quartered (400 grams)

10-12 spring onions, chopped

5 stalks spring onion greens, sliced diagonally

12 garlic cloves, finely chopped

1 tablespoon rice flour

1 cup skimmed milk yogurt, whisked

3 cloves

3 green chillies, seeded and chopped

2 teaspoons coriander powder

Salt to taste

½ teaspoon red chilli powder

½ teaspoon turmeric powder

1 Heat a non-stick pan, add garlic and roast for a minute. Add mushrooms and continue cooking for three to four minutes on low heat. Add rice flour and mix. Add yogurt and cook till the mixture thickens.

2 Add cloves, spring onions and green chillies and continue to cook on low heat for two minutes. Add coriander powder, salt, red chilli powder, turmeric powder and half a cup of water. Cook for two to three minutes. Stir in the spring onion greens. Serve hot.

Veg	Preparation 10 mins	Cooking 15 mins	Serves 4 people

Cabbage
Chana Dal

INGREDIENTS

1 medium cabbage, shredded

¼ cup split Bengal gram (*chana dal*), soaked

1 teaspoon mustard seeds

10-12 curry leaves

4 whole dried red chillies

1 inch ginger, chopped

½ teaspoon turmeric powder

Salt to taste

1 teaspoon *Garam Masala* Powder (pg. 104)

2 tablespoons scraped coconut

1 Drain *chana dal* and boil in approximately one cup of water till just done. Drain and set aside. Heat a non-stick pan. Add mustard seeds and roast for half a minute. Add curry leaves, red chillies and roast for half a minute more. Add ginger and roast for a minute on low heat.

2 Add cabbage and cook, covered, until soft. Add turmeric powder and salt and mix. Add boiled *chana dal* and cook for two minutes. Sprinkle with *garam masala* powder and stir. Garnish with coconut and serve hot.

Veg	Preparation 30 mins	Cooking 20 mins	Serves 4 people

Khumb Hara

Pyaaz

INGREDIENTS

2 cups corn kernels

4 medium green capsicums, seeded, cut into ½ inch pieces

1 teaspoon cumin seeds

2 medium onions, chopped

1 tablespoon ginger paste

1 tablespoon garlic paste

1 teaspoon red chilli powder

1 tablespoon coriander powder

2 teaspoons cumin powder

½ teaspoon turmeric powder

4 medium tomatoes, chopped

Salt to taste

2 teaspoons *Garam Masala* Powder (pg. 104)

1 tablespoon lemon juice

4 tablespoons fresh coriander leaves, chopped

Corn and *Capsicum* Masala

1   Boil corn kernels in three cups of water for about ten minutes. Drain and set aside.

2   Heat a non-stick *kadai* and add cumin seeds. When they begin to change colour, add onions and roast till golden brown.

3   Add ginger paste and garlic paste and cook for two to three minutes. Add red chilli powder, coriander powder, cumin powder and turmeric powder and roast for a few seconds. Add tomatoes and salt and cook, stirring continuously, till the tomatoes turn pulpy. Add half a cup of water, mix well and cook for a minute.

4   Add capsicum and mix well. Finally add boiled corn and *garam masala* powder. Mix and cook on low heat for four to five minutes. Add lemon juice and adjust seasoning.

5   Garnish with coriander leaves. Serve hot.

 Veg
 Preparation 15 mins
 Cooking 20 mins
 Serves 4 people

INGREDIENTS

½ cup cracked wheat (burghul)

8 medium firm red tomatoes

2-3 spring onions, chopped

1 small radish, grated

2 tablespoons raisins (*kishmish*)

2 tablespoons lemon juice

Salt to taste

5-6 black peppercorns, crushed

3 tablespoons fresh parsley, chopped

6-8 lettuce leaves

6-8 fresh mint leaves

Tabbouleh

Stuffed Tomatoes

1   Soak the burghul in boiling hot water for half an hour. Drain, squeeze out excess water and set aside.

2   Cut off the tops of the tomatoes and scoop out the seeds. Reserve the seeds.

3   Mix together burghul, spring onions, radish, raisins, lemon juice, salt, crushed peppercorns, parsley and reserved tomato seeds. Stuff the tomatoes with this filling.

4   Heat sufficient water in a steamer.

5   Place stuffed tomatoes on a perforated plate in the steamer and steam for ten minutes. Remove and set aside to cool for a while.

6   Serve warm, on a bed of lettuce, garnished with roughly torn mint leaves.

 Veg
 Preparation 30 mins
 Cooking 10 mins
 Serves 4 people

65

INGREDIENTS

2 medium potatoes, cut into
  ¼ inch thick oval slices

2 medium onions, halved and
  thickly sliced

2 medium green capsicums, seeded

1 large carrot

100 grams skimmed milk
  cottage cheese (*paneer*)

10 French beans

¼ small cauliflower, separated
  into florets

4 medium tomatoes

1 teaspoon cumin seeds

2 whole dried red chillies,
  broken into half

2 tablespoons vinegar

⅓ cup tomato ketchup

1½ teaspoons red chilli powder

½ teaspoon turmeric powder

2 inches ginger, cut into thin strips

Salt to taste

1 teaspoon *Garam Masala*
  Powder (pg. 104)

2 tablespoons fresh coriander
  leaves, chopped

Vegetable
Jhalfraizee

1 Cut capsicums, carrot, *paneer* and French beans into fingers.

2 Blanch carrot and French beans in two cups of boiling water for two to three minutes. Drain and refresh in cold water. Blanch cauliflower florets in two cups of boiling water for three to four minutes. Drain and refresh in cold water. Purée the tomatoes in a blender.

3 Heat a non-stick pan and roast cumin seeds and red chillies until the seeds change colour. Add vinegar and two tablespoons of water and cook till slightly reduced. Add tomato purée and tomato ketchup and cook for two to three minutes.

4 Add red chilli powder, turmeric powder, ginger, potato slices, salt and one cup of water and cook for two to three minutes.

5 Add onions and capsicums and continue to cook for another two to three minutes.

6 Add carrot, French beans and cauliflower and toss. Add *paneer* and toss gently to mix.

7 Sprinkle *garam masala* powder and serve hot garnished with coriander leaves.

Veg

Preparation
20 mins

Cooking
15 mins

Serves
4 people

Vegetable

Jhalfraizee

Pichki

 Arbi

INGREDIENTS

500 grams colocasia (*arbi*)

½ teaspoon turmeric powder

½ teaspoon red chilli powder

1 teaspoon coriander powder

1 teaspoon carom seeds (*ajwain*)

A pinch of asafoetida

2 green chillies, slit

1 tablespoon lemon juice

2 tablespoons roasted peanuts, coarsely crushed

Salt to taste

2 tablespoons fresh coriander leaves, chopped

1   Scrub and wash the *arbi* well. Boil in sufficient water till done. Drain and peel. Lightly press each *arbi* to flatten. Blend turmeric powder, red chilli powder and coriander powder in one-fourth cup of water. Heat a non-stick pan. Add carom seeds and roast for a few seconds. Add asafoetida and green chillies and stir to mix. Stir in the spice mix.

2   Add half a cup of water and cook till the mixture is reduced by half. Add the flattened *arbi* pieces and salt; mix lightly so that the spices coat the *arbi* evenly. Sprinkle lemon juice and peanuts and mix well. Serve hot garnished with coriander leaves.

Veg | Preparation 15 mins | Cooking 15 mins | Serves 4 people

Masaledar Kaddu

INGREDIENTS

400 grams red pumpkin (*kaddu*)

½ teaspoon fenugreek seeds (*methi dana*)

A pinch of asafoetida

2 green chillies, chopped

Salt to taste

½ teaspoon turmeric powder

1 tablespoon coriander powder

1 inch ginger, cut into thin strips

1½ teaspoons red chilli powder

2 tablespoons sugar

1½ tablespoons lemon juice

2 tablespoons fresh coriander leaves, chopped

1   Peel the pumpkin and cut into one inch pieces. Heat a non-stick pan. Add fenugreek seeds, asafoetida, green chillies and pumpkin pieces and mix. Add salt, turmeric powder, coriander powder, ginger and red chilli powder and mix. Add a little water, cover and cook on moderate heat for ten to fifteen minutes.

2   Add sugar, lemon juice and coriander leaves. Cover and cook on moderate heat for ten minutes till the pumpkin is very soft. Mash the pumpkin gently with the back of a spoon. Serve hot.

Veg | Preparation 15 mins | Cooking 20 mins | Serves 4 people

INGREDIENTS

1 medium carrot, cut into
½ inch cubes

1 large potato, cut into
½ inch cubes

¼ small cauliflower, separated
into florets

10 French beans, cut into
½ inch pieces

½ cup shelled, green peas

1 medium green capsicum, seeded,
cut into ½ inch cubes

2 medium onions, chopped

10-12 curry leaves

2 tomatoes, puréed

1 teaspoon tamarind pulp

Salt to taste

½ cup coconut milk

½ teaspoon *Garam Masala*
Powder (pg. 104)

2 tablespoons fresh coriander
leaves, chopped

FOR THE MASALA PASTE

½ cup scraped coconut

8-10 garlic cloves

1 inch ginger

1 green chilli

2 whole dried red chillies, seeded

2 tablespoons coriander seeds

1 teaspoon cumin seeds

2 tablespoons poppy seeds
(*khuskhus*)

2 tablespoons fennel seeds (*saunf*)

Mixed Vegetable
Kurma

1   Heat a non-stick pan and roast the *masala* ingredients till light brown. Cool and grind to a paste with half a cup of water.

2   Boil carrot, potato, cauliflower, and French beans in salted water till half cooked. Drain and set aside.

3   Heat a non-stick pan, add onions and roast till golden brown. Add curry leaves and *masala* paste. Add half a cup of water and cook for three to four minutes.

4   Add boiled vegetables, green peas, capsicum and tomato purée and bring to a boil. Add tamarind pulp and mix well.

5   Add two and half cups of water and salt. Bring to a boil, lower heat and simmer till the vegetables are cooked and the gravy is thick. Stir in the coconut milk.

6   Sprinkle *garam masala* powder and stir well. Serve hot garnished with coriander leaves.

Chef's Tip: *You can use yogurt in place of the coconut milk. It will add a different, but equally good, flavour to the dish.*

 Veg
 Preparation 20 mins
 Cooking 20 mins
 Serves 4 people

Middle Eastern

Vegetable Stew

INGREDIENTS

2 medium potatoes, peeled,
cut into 1 inch cubes

2 medium carrots, peeled,
cut into 1 inch cubes

1 green capsicum, seeded,
cut into 1 inch pieces

2 medium zucchini, cut into
1 inch pieces

1 small bunch spinach, chopped

½ cup chickpeas (*Kabuli chana*)

3 cups Vegetable Stock (pg. 104)

1 inch fresh ginger, sliced

3-4 cloves

8-10 black peppercorns

1 stalk celery, cut into 1 inch pieces

1 teaspoon cumin powder

A pinch of red chilli powder

Salt to taste

½ teaspoon black pepper powder

10 fresh mint leaves

Middle *Eastern* *Vegetable* Stew

1 Wash and soak chickpeas in sufficient water overnight or for at least six hours. Pressure cook till done and set aside.

2 Heat vegetable stock in a saucepan and bring to a boil.

3 Tie ginger slices, cloves and peppercorns in a piece of muslin and add to the boiling stock.

4 Add boiled chickpeas, potatoes, carrots, celery, cumin powder and red chilli powder. Mix well and cook on medium heat till it begins to boil.

5 Cover and simmer on low heat till all the vegetables are cooked and tender. Add the capsicum, zucchini and spinach and cook for two minutes. Remove the spice bundle and discard.

6 Season with salt and pepper powder and garnish with mint leaves. Serve hot.

 Veg
 Preparation 15 mins
 Cooking 30 mins
 Serves 4 people

INGREDIENTS

8 medium green capsicums

4 medium potatoes, boiled and mashed

1 teaspoon cumin seeds

2 medium onions, chopped

1½ tablespoons ginger-garlic paste

½ teaspoon turmeric powder

2 green chillies, chopped

1½ tablespoons lemon juice

Salt to taste

4 tablespoons fresh coriander leaves, chopped

1 teaspoon *Garam Masala* Powder (pg. 104)

Baked

Stuffed Capsicums

1 Preheat the oven to 180⁰C/350⁰F/Gas Mark 4.

2 Cut off the tops of the capsicums and remove the seeds.

3 Heat a non-stick pan and roast cumin seeds for half a minute. Add onions and roast for a minute. Add ginger-garlic paste and cook for one more minute. Add two tablespoons of water and stir.

4 Add turmeric powder and green chillies and cook for a minute. Add the mashed potatoes and mix well. Add lemon juice to moisten potato mixture. Add salt, coriander leaves and *garam masala* powder and mix well.

5 Stuff the potato mixture into the capsicum cups and arrange them on a baking tray. Bake for ten to fifteen minutes or till the tops turn light golden brown.

6 Take out of the oven and serve with a gravy or sauce of your choice.

Veg

Preparation
15 mins

Cooking
30 mins

Serves
4 people

INGREDIENTS

1 medium carrot, cut into
½ inch cubes

½ small cauliflower, separated
into florets

½ small broccoli, separated
into florets

10-12 French beans, cut into
½ inch diamonds

½ cup shelled green peas

5 cups skimmed milk

6 tablespoons wholewheat flour
(*atta*)

Salt to taste

5-6 black peppercorns, crushed

¼ cup brown breadcrumbs

2 tablespoons fresh parsley, chopped

Mixed *Vegetables*

in a White *Sauce*

1   Preheat the oven to 180ºC/350ºF/Gas Mark 4.

2   Blanch carrot, cauliflower florets, broccoli florets, French beans and green peas separately in boiling water for few minutes. Drain, refresh in cold water and set aside.

3   Boil milk and cool. Take a heavy bottomed non-stick pan and dry roast the wheat flour on low heat till fragrant. Add milk gradually, whisking continuously, so that no lumps form. Season with salt and crushed peppercorns. Remove from heat when the sauce thickens, strain and set aside to cool.

4   Mix all the boiled vegetables together.

5   Take an oven-proof glass bowl. Spread one third of the white sauce on the base. Arrange half the vegetables on it. Cover with half the remaining white sauce, followed by remaining vegetables. Finally top the vegetables with the remaining white sauce. Sprinkle fresh brown breadcrumbs.

6   Bake for ten to fifteen minutes.

7   Serve hot garnished with parsley.

 Veg
 Preparation 20 mins
 Cooking 25 mins
 Serves 4 people

INGREDIENTS

4 large potatoes

1 cup baked beans

1 bay leaf

1 medium onion, chopped

6 garlic cloves, chopped

1 tablespoon tomato ketchup

1 teaspoon sea salt

¼ teaspoon black pepper powder

Jacket *Potatoes*

with *Baked*

Beans Stuffing

1 Parboil potatoes with the skins on. Drain, cool and halve. Scoop out the centres leaving a thick shell around.

2 Preheat the oven to 200⁰C/400⁰F/Gas Mark 6.

3 Heat a non-stick pan, add bay leaf, onion and garlic and cook till the onion turns a light brown.

4 Add tomato ketchup and mix well.

5 Add baked beans, sea salt and pepper powder, stir and bring the mixture to a boil.

6 Cool slightly. Fill the scooped out potato halves with the baked beans mixture. Arrange the potatoes on a baking tray and bake for fifteen to twenty minutes.

7 Serve hot.

Note: The scooped out portion of the potatoes can be used in some other dish.

 Veg

 Preparation 15 mins

 Cooking 30 mins

 Serves 4 people

Jacket Potatoes with

Baked Beans Stuffing

INGREDIENTS

1½ cups Basmati rice, soaked

4 medium carrots, cut into
½ inch pieces

10-12 cauliflower florets

15 French beans, cut into
½ inch pieces

1 cup shelled green peas

A few strands of saffron (*kesar*)

¼ cup milk

4 large onions, sliced

1½ cups skimmed milk yogurt

1½ tablespoons ginger-garlic paste

4-5 green chillies, finely chopped

1 tablespoon coriander powder

1 teaspoon turmeric powder

1 tablespoon red chilli powder

¾ teaspoon *Garam Masala* Powder
(pg. 104)

Salt to taste

2 green cardamoms

1 black cardamom

4 cloves

½ inch cinnamon

1 bay leaf

2 tablespoons fresh coriander leaves,
chopped

2 tablespoons fresh mint leaves,
chopped

A few drops of *kewra* essence (optional)

2 inches ginger, cut into thin strips

Mixed *Vegetable* Biryani

1   Soak saffron in warm milk. Heat a non-stick pan, add onions and roast till brown. Set aside. Blanch all the vegetables separately. Drain and refresh in cold water.

2   In a bowl mix the vegetables with yogurt, ginger-garlic paste, green chillies, coriander powder, turmeric powder, red chilli powder, half the *garam masala* powder, salt and half the browned onions. Transfer the mixture into a deep pan.

3   Drain the rice and boil in four cups of boiling salted water with green cardamoms, black cardamom, cloves, cinnamon and bay leaf until three-fourth done. Drain excess water. Spread the rice over the vegetables in the deep pan.

4   Sprinkle saffron soaked in milk, coriander leaves, mint leaves, *kewra* essence, ginger strips, remaining *garam masala* powder and remaining browned onions over the rice.

5   Cover the pan with aluminium foil and cover tightly with the lid so that the steam does not escape.

6   Place the pan over medium heat and cook for around fifteen to twenty minutes or till the rice and vegetables are done. Serve hot with a *raita* of your choice.

Veg   Preparation 20 mins   Making 40 mins   Serves 4 people

INGREDIENTS

250 grams penne

5 medium tomatoes

6 garlic cloves, crushed

2 medium onions, sliced

1 teaspoon crushed red chillies

1 tablespoon oregano

Salt to taste

5-6 basil leaves

Penne *Arrabbiata*

1 Blanch tomatoes, peel, remove seeds and coarsely chop. Cook penne in plenty of salted boiling water, drain, refresh in cold water and set aside.

2 Heat a non-stick pan, add garlic and roast until light brown. Add onions, roast until transluscent and then add crushed red chillies, oregano and tomatoes.

3 Cook for about five minutes on low heat. Add salt and mix well. Add penne and roughly torn basil leaves and toss lightly. Serve hot.

| Veg | Preparation 15 mins | Cooking 10 mins | Serves 4 people |

INGREDIENTS

1½ cups risotto rice

1 medium onion, chopped

4 garlic cloves, chopped

3 cups Vegetable Stock (pg. 104)

Salt to taste

½ teaspoon black pepper powder

2 medium carrots, sliced

2 cups skimmed milk

7-8 black peppercorns, crushed

1 teaspoon dried basil

5-6 French beans, cut into
   1 inch pieces

1 medium green capsicum, seeded
   cut into ½ inch pieces

5-6 fresh button mushrooms, sliced

No-Cheese Risotto

1 Heat a non-stick pan, add onion and garlic and cook till transparent. Add rice, stir and roast for two to three minutes. Add three cups of hot stock, salt and pepper powder and mix well. Add carrots, cover and cook till the rice is half-done.

2 Add milk, crushed peppercorns and dried basil. Cook till half the milk has been absorbed. Add French beans, capsicum and mushrooms and cook till the vegetables are soft. Remove from heat and serve hot.

Chef's Tip: *Traditionally arborio rice is used to make risotto. But you can also use ukda chawal (parboiled rice).*

| Veg | Preparation 15 mins | Cooking 25 mins | Serves 4 people |

Penne
Arrabbiata

Brown Rice
Vegetable
Pilaf

INGREDIENTS

1½ cups brown rice

2 medium carrots, cut into
½ inch cubes

10-12 French beans, cut into
½ inch pieces

¼ medium cauliflower, separated into
small florets

6-7 medium fresh button mushrooms,
(optional) halved

½ cup green peas, shelled

1 bay leaf

2-3 cloves

1 teaspoon cumin seeds

1 inch cinnamon

2 green chillies, slit

Salt to taste

2 tablespoons fresh coriander
leaves, finely chopped

Brown Rice

Vegetable Pilaf

1 Soak brown rice in four to five cups of water for two
hours. Drain and set aside.

2 Heat a deep non-stick pan, add bay leaf, cloves,
cumin seeds and cinnamon and roast for a few
seconds or till fragrant. Add drained rice and roast
for one to two minutes more. Add four cups of water
and bring to a boil.

3 Add carrots, French beans, cauliflower, mushrooms
and green chillies. Stir and bring to a boil. Add salt
and mix. Lower heat, cover and cook till almost done.

4 Add green peas and mix gently. Cover and cook
till done.

5 Serve hot, garnished with fresh coriander leaves.

Note: Brown rice is available at health food stores.

 Veg
 Preparation 2 hrs
 Cooking 25 mins
 Serves 4 people

INGREDIENTS

- 1½ cups Basmati rice
- 1 medium carrot, cut into ½ inch diamonds
- 10 French beans, ½ inch diamonds
- ¼ small cauliflower, separated into florets
- 2 medium tomatoes, chopped
- 1 bay leaf
- ½ teaspoon cumin seeds
- 2 inches cinnamon
- 2 black cardamoms
- 1 inch ginger, chopped
- 7-8 Madras (sambhar) onions, peeled and halved
- Salt to taste
- 7-8 black peppercorns, crushed
- ½ teaspoon red chilli powder
- ½ teaspoon *Garam Masala* Powder (pg. 104)
- 1 tablespoon lemon juice
- 3 tablespoons fresh coriander leaves, chopped

Mixed **Vegetables**

and Tomato

Pulao

1 Soak rice in three cups of water for half an hour. Drain and set aside.

2 Heat a deep non-stick pan and dry roast bay leaf, cumin seeds, cinnamon and black cardamoms till fragrant. Add ginger, Madras onions, tomatoes and salt to taste. Stir and cook for two to three minutes.

3 Add three cups of water and stir. Bring to a boil and add carrot, French beans, cauliflower, rice, crushed peppercorns, red chilli powder and *garam masala* powder and stir gently, but continuously for three to four minutes.

4 Adjust salt. Cover and cook on low heat till done. Add lemon juice and mix.

5 Serve hot, garnished with coriander leaves.

 Veg
 Preparation 30 mins
 Cooking 15 mins
 Serves 4 people

INGREDIENTS

1 medium red capsicum,
  seeded and quartered

5 medium tomatoes,
  seeded and quartered

5-6 garlic cloves , chopped fine

Salt to taste

2 teaspoons sugar

2 tablespoons lemon juice

1 sprig fresh parsley

Roasted *Capsicum*
and Tomato *Dip*

1 Preheat oven to 180°C/350°F/Gas Mark 4.

2 Arrange red capsicum and tomato together with garlic on a baking tray. Sprinkle with salt.

3 Bake for twenty to twenty-five minutes and allow to cool. When cool, peel capsicum and tomato wedges and chop.

4 Heat a non-stick pan and roast garlic for a minute. Add capsicum and tomatoes and cook for two minutes. Add more salt, if necessary and the sugar. Mix well.

5 Cook for another two minutes and add lemon juice. Mix again. Serve garnished with a sprig of parsley.

Note: When in a hurry, purée baked capsicums, tomatoes and garlic without peeling and cook till done.

 Veg Preparation 10 mins Cooking 35 mins Serves 4 people

Chholay
Biryani

INGREDIENTS

1½ cups Basmati rice

1 cup chickpeas (*Kabuli chana*)

2 tablespoons tea leaves

Salt to taste

5-6 green cardamoms

2-3 bay leaves

2-3 cloves

1½ cups skimmed milk yogurt

1 teaspoon ginger paste

1 inch ginger, cut into thin strips

½ cup fresh mint leaves

1 teaspoon green chilli paste

1 teaspoon red chilli powder

1 teaspoon turmeric powder

1 teaspoon *Garam Masala* Powder (pg. 104)

1 teaspoon garlic paste

A few strands of saffron

1 tablespoon skimmed milk

A few drops of *kewra* water

¼ cup fresh coriander leaves, chopped

Chholay

Biryani

1 Soak *Kabuli chana* overnight or for six hours in four cups of water. Drain and pressure cook in four cups of fresh water with salt and tea leaves tied in a piece of muslin, till tender. Remove the muslin bag and drain chickpeas.

2 Marinate boiled chickpeas in yogurt, ginger paste, ginger strips, half the mint leaves, green chilli paste, red chilli powder, turmeric powder, *garam masala* powder and garlic paste.

3 Soak rice in three cups of water for about half an hour. Drain. Boil four cups of water in a deep pan with salt, green cardamoms, bay leaves and cloves. Add rice and cook till half done. Drain.

4 Dissolve saffron in warm milk and mix in *kewra* water. Place the marinated chickpeas in a deep non-stick pan.

5 Spread cooked rice over the chickpeas evenly. Sprinkle dissolved saffron and half the coriander leaves over the rice.

6 Cover the pan tightly and cook on low heat for fifteen minutes or till rice is done. Serve hot, garnished with remaining coriander and mint leaves.

Chef's Tip: *You can use chholay masala to add more flavour to this biryani.*

 Veg
 Preparation 90 mins
 Cooking 30 mins
 Serves 4 people

INGREDIENTS

½ cup whole green gram (*sabut moong*)

Salt to taste

2 tablespoons gram flour (*besan*)

1½ cups skimmed milk yogurt

¼ teaspoon turmeric powder

1 teaspoon ginger paste

1 teaspoon green chilli paste

1 teaspoon sugar

½ teaspoon mustard seeds

¼ teaspoon fenugreek seeds
(*methi dana*)

½ teaspoon cumin seeds

8-10 curry leaves

2 whole dried red chillies

3-4 cloves

1 inch cinnamon

A pinch of asafoetida

2 tablespoons fresh coriander leaves,
chopped

Khatte
Moong

1 Soak *moong* in two cups of water for about an hour. Drain, add two cups of water and salt and boil till soft.

2 Whisk together *besan* and yogurt to make a smooth mixture. Add turmeric powder, ginger paste, green chilli paste, sugar and three cups of water and mix well.

3 Transfer the mixture to a pan and cook, stirring continuously, till the *kadhi* is moderately thick. Add salt to taste.

4 Heat a small non-stick pan and add mustard seeds, fenugreek seeds, cumin seeds, curry leaves, red chillies, cloves, cinnamon and asafoetida. Roast on medium heat till fragrant. Add it to the *kadhi* and mix well.

5 Stir in the boiled *moong* and adjust seasoning. Simmer for two minutes.

6 Serve hot garnished with coriander leaves.

Veg | Preparation 15 mins | Cooking 20 mins | Serves 4 people

Peshawari

Chana

INGREDIENTS

1 cup chickpeas (*Kabuli chana*), soaked overnight

2 teaspoons tea leaves

Salt to taste

1 medium onion, finely sliced

2 tablespoons ginger-garlic-green chilli paste

1 cup tomato purée

1½ tablespoons *chana masala*

2 tablespoons coriander leaves, chopped

4 green chillies, slit

---

1 Tie the tea leaves in a small piece of muslin. Drain and boil chickpeas with three cups of water, salt and tea leaves in a pressure cooker till soft. When done drain and remove the pouch. Reserve the cooking liquid.

2 Heat a non-stick *kadai*. Add onion and roast till golden brown.

3 Add ginger-garlic-green chilli paste and continue to cook for two more minutes.

4 Add tomato purée and cook for five minutes.

5 Add boiled chickpeas, reserved cooking liquid and cook for five minutes.

6 Take the pan off the heat and sprinkle *chana masala*. Mix well.

7 Garnish with coriander leaves and green chillies and serve hot.

INGREDIENTS

½ cup split Bengal gram (*chana dal*)

½ small bottle gourd (*lauki*), peeled, cut into 1 inch cubes

Salt to taste

½ teaspoon turmeric powder

½ teaspoon cumin seeds

2 green chillies, chopped

A pinch of asafoetida

½ teaspoon red chilli powder

2 teaspoons coriander powder

2 medium tomatoes, chopped

½ teaspoon *Garam Masala* Powder (Pg. 104)

¼ teaspoon sugar

2 teaspoons lemon juice

2 tablespoons fresh coriander leaves, chopped

Lauki Chana

1 Soak *chana dal* in one and half cups of water for an hour. Drain.

2 Boil *chana dal* and *lauki* with salt, turmeric powder and three cups of water till done. Mash lightly with the back of a rounded spoon and mix well. Set aside.

3 Heat a non-stick pan. Add cumin seeds, green chillies and asafoetida and cook for a minute. Add red chilli powder, coriander powder and two tablespoons of water and cook till fragrant.

4 Add tomatoes and cook till they soften.

5 Add cooked *chana dal* and *lauki* and stir to mix. Add *garam masala* powder, sugar and more salt if necessary. Simmer for two minutes.

6 Add lemon juice and stir. Garnish with coriander leaves and serve hot.

Veg | Preparation 1 hr | Cooking 25 mins | Serves 4 people

Lauki Chana
Dal

Tamatar
ki Kadhi

Beetroot
Raita

Tamatar  *ki Kadhi*

INGREDIENTS

12 small tomatoes, puréed

4 teaspoons gram flour (*besan*)

½ teaspoon turmeric powder

1 teaspoon red chilli powder

Salt to taste

1 teaspoon sugar

½ teaspoon mustard seeds

A pinch of asafoetida

½ teaspoon cumin seeds

5-6 curry leaves

4-5 whole red chillies

2 tablespoons fresh coriander leaves, chopped

1 Mix tomato purée, gram flour, turmeric powder, red chilli powder, salt and sugar. Whisk till well blended. Stir in two cups of water.

2 Heat a deep non-stick pan and roast mustard seeds, asafoetida, cumin seeds, curry leaves and whole red chillies till fragrant.

3 Add the tomato mixture and bring to a boil. Reduce heat and simmer for ten minutes.

4 Serve hot, garnished with coriander leaves.

Veg — Preparation 15 mins — Cooking 15 mins — Serves 4 people

Beetroot *Raita*

INGREDIENTS

1 small beetroot

2 cups skimmed milk yogurt, whisked

1 teaspoon roasted cumin powder

½ teaspoon red chilli powder

1 tablespoon fresh coriander leaves, finely chopped

Salt to taste

1 Boil, peel and grate beetroot. Chill in the refrigerator.

2 Add roasted cumin powder, red chilli powder, fresh coriander leaves and salt to yogurt and mix well.

3 Add chilled beetroot and mix gently.

4 Serve chilled.

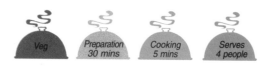

Veg — Preparation 30 mins — Cooking 5 mins — Serves 4 people

INGREDIENTS

2 cups wholewheat flour (*atta*) +
extra for dusting

1 medium bunch spinach,
(350 grams) chopped

100 grams skimmed milk cottage
cheese (*chhenna/paneer*)

½ cup skimmed milk yogurt,
whisked + to serve

1 small onion, finely chopped

½ teaspoon carom seeds (*ajwain*)

2 tablespoons fresh coriander leaves,
chopped

2 tablespoons fresh mint leaves

2 green chillies, chopped

½ teaspoon cumin powder

1 teaspoon *chaat masala*

1 teaspoon *Garam Masala* Powder
(pg. 104)

Salt to taste

Palak and

Chhenna Parantha

1   Take wholewheat flour in a deep bowl.

2   Add remaining ingredients and knead into a medium
soft dough with sufficient water. Cover and rest the
dough for fifteen minutes.

3   Divide the dough into twelve equal portions and
shape into balls.

4   Roll out into thick *paranthas*. Heat a *tawa* and roast
paranthas on moderate heat on both sides till brown
and crisp.

5   Serve hot with skimmed milk yogurt.

Veg   Preparation 15 mins   Cooking 20 mins   Serves 4 people

INGREDIENTS

2 cups wholewheat flour (*atta*)

Salt to taste

¼ teaspoon turmeric powder

1 teaspoon cumin powder

1 teaspoon ginger-green chilli paste

1 teaspoon dried fenugreek leaves
 (*kasoori methi*)

Methi
Khakhra

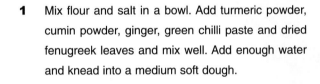

1 Mix flour and salt in a bowl. Add turmeric powder, cumin powder, ginger, green chilli paste and dried fenugreek leaves and mix well. Add enough water and knead into a medium soft dough.

2 Divide the dough into twelve equal balls. Roll out each ball into very thin, round *chapatis*.

3 Heat a non-stick *tawa*, put a *chapati* on it and roast on low heat. Turn and press the *chapati* with a wooden press. Continue pressing and turning till the *khakra* is evenly cooked on both the sides.

4 The *khakra* is done when it is light brown and crisp. Take off the heat, allow to cool and store in an airtight container handling it carefully as it is very crisp and may break.

 Veg

 Preparation 10 mins

 Cooking 20 mins

 Serves 4 people

Palak & Chhenna

Parantha

Methi
Khakhra

Methi
Makai

Parantha

Methi Makai

Parantha

INGREDIENTS

2 cups wholewheat flour (*atta*)

½ cup fresh fenugreek leaves (*methi*), chopped

½ cup corn kernels (*makai*), boiled and crushed

Salt to taste

1 small onion, chopped

1 medium potato, boiled, peeled and mashed

2 tablespoons fresh coriander leaves, chopped

2 green chillies, chopped

½ teaspoon carom seeds (*ajwain*)

1 tablespoon lemon juice

1   Mix wholewheat flour and salt and knead with enough water into a soft dough. Divide into eight equal portions. Cover with a damp cloth for about fifteen minutes.

2   Heat a non-stick *kadai*. Add onion, corn kernels and fenugreek leaves and cook till dry. Spread on a plate to cool.

3   When cool, mix in the mashed potato. Add coriander leaves, green chillies, carom seeds, lemon juice and salt and mix well. Divide into eight equal portions.

4   Roll out one portion of dough into a small *puri*, place one portion of stuffing in the centre, gather the edges together and roll into a ball.

5   Roll out the ball into a *parantha* about five inches in diameter. Do the same with the rest of the dough and stuffing.

6   Heat a non-stick *tawa*, place a *parantha* on it and roast till light golden specks appear. Turn over and roast the other side.

7   Serve hot with yogurt.

Veg

Preparation
20 mins

Cooking
15 mins

Serves
4 people

Date *and Tamarind*
Chutney

INGREDIENTS

15-20 dates (*khajur*)

1 cup tamarind pulp

2 teaspoons cumin seeds

¼ teaspoon fennel seeds (*saunf*)

½ cup jaggery, grated

2 teaspoons red chilli powder

1 teaspoon dried ginger powder (*soonth*)

1 teaspoon black salt

Salt to taste

1 Wash dates, stone and chop roughly. Dry roast cumin seeds and fennel seeds. Cool slightly and grind to a powder. Mix together dates, tamarind pulp, cumin and fennel powder, jaggery, red chilli powder, dried ginger powder, black salt, salt and four cups of water.

2 Cook on moderate heat till the mixture comes to a boil, lower heat and simmer for six to eight minutes, or till the chutney is thick. Cool and serve, or store for later use.

Veg | Preparation 10 mins | Cooking 10 mins | Serves 4 people

Green Mango
and Onion Chutney

INGREDIENTS

3 medium green, unripe mangoes, peeled, stoned and chopped

2 medium onions, grated

4-6 green chillies, chopped

1 tablespoon pomegranate seeds (*anardana*)

2 tablespoons lemon juice

½ teaspoon black salt

Salt to taste

½ teaspoon sugar

1 Put the green mangoes, green chillies, pomegranate seeds, lemon juice, salt and sugar into a blender and blend till smooth.

2 Adjust the consistency by adding water. Squeeze the grated onion to remove excess juice and add to the chutney.

Veg | Preparation 10 mins | Cooking nil | Serves 4 people

Green Mango and Onion

Chutney

Dhania Pudina

Parantha

INGREDIENTS

2 cups wholewheat flour (*atta*)

¼ cup fresh coriander leaves, chopped

¼ cup fresh mint leaves, chopped

Salt to taste

2 teaspoons *chaat masala*

½ cup skimmed milk yogurt

Dhania

Pudina

Parantha

1   Place the wholewheat flour and salt in a bowl. Add coriander leaves, mint leaves and enough water to make a soft dough. Cover and rest the dough for twenty to twenty-five minutes.

2   Divide the dough into eight equal portions and shape into balls.

3   Mix yogurt and *chaat masala*.

4   Roll out each ball into a medium-sized *chapati*. Spread with a tablespoon of the yogurt mixture. Fold the *chapati* like a fan and twist it back into the form of a ball. Set aside for five minutes.

5   Roll out each portion into a *parantha* of five to seven inches diameter. Cook on a hot non-stick *tawa* till both sides are a light golden brown.

6   Before serving, crush the *paranthas* lightly between your palms to open out the layers.

 Veg

 Preparation 25 mins

 Cooking 25 mins

 Serves 4 people

INGREDIENTS

2 medium bunches (350 grams each)
spinach

1 green chilli

2 cups skimmed milk yogurt

Black salt to taste

1 teaspoon roasted cumin powder

Salt to taste

Palak

Raita

1 Blanch one bunch of spinach in boiling water, drain and refresh in cold water. Drain, squeeze out excess water and purée with one green chilli in a blender. Shred the remaining spinach.

2 Whisk yogurt and add spinach purée, black salt and roasted cumin powder. Mix well and chill in the refrigerator.

3 Heat a non-stick pan. Add shredded spinach and cook over high heat for three to four minutes, stirring continuously.

4 Season with salt and mix well. Continue to cook on high heat till the spinach is almost dry. Take the pan off the heat and cool.

5 Mix the spinach with the flavoured yogurt just before serving. Adjust salt and serve chilled.

Veg

Preparation
10 mins

Cooking
10 mins

Serves
4 people

Chhannar
Payesh

INGREDIENTS

- ½ cup *chhenna (paneer)*, made from skimmed cow's milk
- 1 litre (5 cups) skimmed milk
- ½ cup sugar
- 5-6 almonds, blanched and chopped
- 7-8 pistachios, blanched and chopped

1 Boil milk, lower heat and simmer till reduced to half the original quantity. Add sugar and cook till it dissolves.

2 Mash *chhenna* in a bowl. Add it to the milk. Simmer for two minutes. Sprinkle chopped nuts and serve cold.

Chef's Tip: If cow's milk chhenna is not available use chhenna made from buffalo's milk. I recommend chhenna made from cow's milk because it is low in fat.

Veg — Preparation 15 mins — Cooking 30 mins — Serves 4 people

Gajar
ki Kheer

INGREDIENTS

- 2 medium carrots, grated
- 1 litre (5 cups) skimmed milk
- ¹/₃ cup sugar
- ¼ teaspoon green cardamom powder
- 2 tablespoons raisins (*kishmish*)

1 Bring the milk to a boil, reduce heat and simmer till it is reduced to three-fourth its original volume.

2 Add carrots and cook on low heat for about fifteen to twenty minutes or till the carrots are completely cooked. Add sugar and cook, stirring occasionally, till sugar dissolves.

3 Add green cardamom powder and stir well. Serve garnished with raisins.

Veg — Preparation 10 mins — Cooking 30 mins — Serves 4 people

INGREDIENTS

6 tablespoons vermicelli (*sevian*)

10-15 strands saffron

1½ litres (7½ cups) skimmed milk

8 tablespoons sugar

20 raisins (*kishmish*)

1 teaspoon green cardamom powder

1 tablespoon almond slivers, toasted

Zafrani

Sevian

1 Heat a non-stick pan and roast vermicelli on moderate heat till lightly browned.

2 Pour milk into a deep pan and bring to a boil. Lower heat and simmer till reduced to half the quantity.

3 Add sugar and cook till it dissolves. Add vermicelli and raisins and cook for two minutes.

4 Take the pan off the heat. Add saffron and green cardamom powder and stir well.

5 Serve hot or cold, decorated with toasted almond slivers.

 Veg

 Preparation 10 mins

 Cooking 45 mins

 Serves 4 people

Zafrani

Sevian

INGREDIENTS

½ cup semolina (*suji/rawa*)

1½ litres (7½ cups) skimmed milk

7-8 strands saffron

½ cup sugar

2 tablespoons *charoli* (*chironjee*)

20 almonds, blanched and slivered

Suji

Kheer

1 Roast *suji* in a thick-bottomed pan on low heat for fifteen minutes or till light brown.

2 Soak saffron in one tablespoon of milk.

3 Bring remaining milk to a boil and simmer on moderate heat till reduced to one litre.

4 Add thickened milk to *suji*, stirring continuously to prevent lumps from forming.

5 Cook on high heat till it comes to a boil. Add sugar and simmer for two to three minutes.

6 Add saffron and stir well.

7 Decorate with *charoli* and almond slivers and serve hot or cold.

 Veg

 Preparation 15 mins

 Cooking 25 mins

 Serves 4 people

Pineapple

Yogurt Fool

INGREDIENTS

½ medium fresh pineapple, cut into small cubes

½ cup sugar

1 inch cinnamon

½ cup drained skimmed milk yogurt

1 Mix pineapple, sugar and cinnamon in a pan and stew for thirty minutes. Set aside to cool.

2 Remove pineapple pieces and mix with drained yogurt. Process together in a blender. Chill in the refrigerator. Serve chilled.

| Veg | Preparation 10 mins | Cooking 40 mins | Serves 4 people |

Sitaphal

Basoondi

INGREDIENTS

1½ litres (7½ cups) skimmed milk

1 cup sitaphal (custard apple) pulp

½ cup sugar

½ teaspoon green cardamom powder

10-12 pistachios, sliced

1 tablespoon *charoli* (*chironjee*)

10-12 almonds, blanched and slivered

3-4 rose petals (optional)

1 Bring the milk to a boil in a heavy bottomed pan on high heat. Lower heat and simmer for half an hour. Keep stirring so that the milk does not burn and stick to the bottom of the pan.

2 When the milk reduces to half the original quantity, add sugar. Simmer for five more minutes. Take the pan off the heat and set aside to cool. When cool, add custard apple, green cardamom powder, sliced pistachios and *charoli*. Transfer to a serving bowl and garnish with almond slivers and rose petals. Serve cold.

| Veg | Preparation 10 mins | Cooking 30 mins | Serves 4 people |

Anjeer
ka Meetha

Sitaphal
Basoondi

INGREDIENTS

250 grams dried figs (*anjeer*)

250 grams dried, seedless dates

¼ cup skimmed milk powder

4-5 almonds, roasted and slivered

Anjeer

ka Meetha

1   Soak figs in three cups of water for three to four hours. Boil them in the same water in which they were soaked, for three to five minutes.

2   Take the pan off the heat, drain the figs and cool slightly. Reserve some figs and purée the rest. Chop the reserved figs.

3   Chop dates roughly and soak in two cups of hot water for fifteen to twenty minutes. Drain and purée.

4   Mix the two purées and add skimmed milk powder. Mix well and cook on low heat for fifteen to twenty minutes or till well blended.

5   Add the chopped figs and simmer for another two to three minutes.

6   Serve garnished with almond slivers.

 Veg
 Preparation 3 hrs
 Cooking 25 mins
 Serves 4 people

Annexure

Goda Masala Powder

Roast 1 cup coriander seeds, 2 tablespoons cumin seeds, ¼ cup stone flower, 6 two-inch sticks cinnamon, 16 green cardamoms, 25 cloves, ¾ teaspoon caraway seeds, 10-12 black peppercorns, 10-12 bay leaves, 1 teaspoon *nagkeshar,* 2 blades mace, 3 tablespoons dried coconut, grated, 1 teaspoon sesame seeds, 3 whole red chillies and 1 teaspoon asafoetida separately one by one. Cool and grind to a fine powder. Bottle. Makes 100 grams of *goda masala* powder.

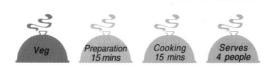

Garam Masala Powder

Lightly dry roast 10-12 blades of mace, 8-10 one-inch sticks of cinnamon, 25 cloves, 25 green cardamoms, 10-12 black cardamoms, 2 nutmegs, 8-10 bay leaves, 8 teaspoons cumin seeds and 4 teaspoons black peppercorns one by one. Cool and grind to a fine powder. Bottle.

Vegetable Stock

Peel, wash and chop 1 onion, ½ medium carrot, 2-3 inch stalk celery and 2-3 garlic cloves. Place in a pan with 1 bay leaf, 5-6 peppercorns, 2-3 cloves and five cups of water and bring to a boil. Lower heat and simmer for fifteen minutes and strain. Cool and store in a refrigerator till further use.

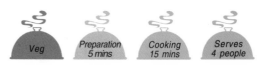